A Season For All Men

A SEASON
FOR ALL MEN

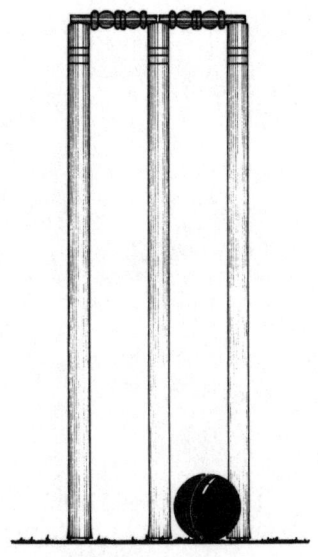

E. VALENTINE JOYCE

THE
BOOK GUILD LIMITED
Lewes

*To my late Mother, whom I sorely disappointed in life,
yet was ever forgiven.*

The Book Guild Limited
Temple House, 25 High Street,
Lewes, Sussex

First published 1985
© E. Valentine Joyce 1985

Set in Linotron Plantin & Helvetica

Typesetting by Central Southern Typesetters
Eastbourne 23373/21195

Printed in Great Britain by
Paradigm Print,
Gateshead, Tyne and Wear

ISBN 0 86332 112 7

Contents

Foreword

Let me say at the outset that these ramblings are purely the reflections of an ordinary spectator. They constitute a review of times past as seen from the 'sixpenny seats', and are meant to appeal to laymen of like kind. The layman, of course, need not be unenlightened. Many a man whose nine not out in a parent's match remains forever a cherished memory, has nevertheless a keen insight into the game — from the stand. And it is with those that one hopes to share great moments.

'Cricketer's cricket' is something quite other, and a province into which I am hardly qualified to venture. Nor would such first-hand knowledge serve my purpose here, where we have set out to recall the best from the spectator's point of view. For the players, cricket does not need to be bright, nor always entertaining. Even on the dullest days, when to we tyros round the ring, proceedings have lost all meaning, have no doubt there is something going on out there. Something tactical, technical — something in the player's minds that we do not fully appreciate. As on that exasperating last day when one waits patiently for the declaration that would make a game of it, only for one side to bat out for a tame draw. You can be sure there is method in it somewhere. Test captains, as we well know, are not renowned for their bold sense of adventure. With the rubber at stake, better to live and fight another day. And so on. All that we can safely leave to the experts, in whose ranks, as I say, I scarcely number.

Like you, perhaps, my cricket never aspired to the heights such devotion surely merited, and at this advanced age, I am unlikely to know what it is to face a Tyson charging in from the pavilion end. Or, as in dreams of younger days, to dive full-length to take that blinder in the gully. (Once, when lost in blissful reverie, I involuntarily shot out a hand, and quickly found myself on the bedroom floor. Even for mere followers, cricket can be a dangerous game.)

There is an old saying, however, that runs, 'Those who can, do; those who can't, teach'. Which might equally read, 'Those who can't, write'. This one can do without suffering any of the disappointments one meets on the pitch each Saturday, and moreover in better company. At a stroke of the pen, you can be at one with the greats, transported when and wherever you choose. Delivered thus, I have set out to recapture a few of the golden summers, safe in the knowledge that others will have bathed in their glow as well. In so doing I have endeavoured to mix a blend of drama, nostalgia and humour — those essential ingredients of our great summer game. We shall be spanning a period of some fifty-three years, years in which moods and attitudes change but memorable cricket remains a constant. But 11.30 approaches; do you hear the call of 'play'?

I – Causes and Effects

"That was a great year!" How often has one heard that phrase when talk turns to cricket past? But how do we, King Willow's loyal subjects, truly define a summer spectacular, a season beau ideal? Opinions differ, of course, though one feels there will be much common ground in their formation. It is doubtful anyway, if we have yet seen the year that conformed to every pundit's criteria, or indeed could ever do so; the best might still want for absolute perfection. But that is another matter. The fact is, we can all point to summers that remain vivid to the mind, summers which can rightly be deemed 'vintage'. Now just what elevates them so?

There is, of course, no definitive answer. We can be certain, however, that they are memorable not on the strength of one prominent feature, but on many, on a rare convergence of all we find best in the game — or at least, something approaching that exalted ideal. For reasons of age alone, our favoured years may not correspond, yet I venture to suggest that much the same ingredients motivate each of us. In fact, it's all Lords to a long-stop, that for most cricket-lovers a season of distinction is merely an embodiment of fairly basic factors. For example: Is our lasting impression of sun-drenched days and hard wickets? Were there players of rare charisma, given to attacking cricket; mighty achievements with a genuine record or two? Was it entertaining in every sense; a fair contest of bat and ball?

No doubt some would insist that strength-in-depth is also a prerequisite, yet while obviously desirable, this has not always proved essential. As one says, one seldom, if ever, finds circumstances made wholly to order. But to continue.

In the above short-list, favourable elements appear as the first consideration. This is no accident. Without sunshine, it is no sort of season at all. While you could find exceptions to the rule, in broad terms, cricket on dull days just isn't cricket.

The second priority — players in a class of their own — should brook little argument. Cricket is only so good as its practitioners, and needs the true individuals to set it apart — whatever the purists might say. We talk much of team spirit in our hallowed game — playing for the side, pulling together and suchlike, precepts one grows up with, and which appeal to many of our better instincts. Noble sentiments, of course, sound in principle, yet from the spectator's angle, one thinks, not strictly valid. After all, whilst all freely acknowledge the healthy conception of team effort, do we still not seek idols to worship, and flock to wherever they may play? I shall no doubt be thrown into the Tower on charges of subversive preaching, but I nevertheless suggest that in this respect, the player counts for more than the side. Not the man in himself you understand — that would never do — but in the sense that it is largely the presence of famous names that draws the crowds. Did not the prospect of W.G. batting warrant a 100 per cent surcharge at the gate?

Further proof of this can be seen in our willingness to watch just isolated passages of a game, when the result would seem to be of less interest than the play overall. Few, for example, would pay to witness the first half of a soccer match or one set of tennis, yet the majority of cricket's faithful happily settle for, maybe, one day of a Test — and that not usually the last. They see it not as a five-part serial, but as a series of tableaux, each a spectacle in its own right, one performer giving way to another in a pageant of solo turns. Of course, one may see a tense duel or a fruitful partnership, involving co-artists, but whatever the action, it will be viewed as a singular event. Who cares about the finish, when 'yours' was, perhaps, the best day of all. A Thursday crowd at Headingley, say, is there for no other reason than to embody Yorkshire lusting after its favourite son's century. It is thus the world over.

Without labouring the point, it comes to this. Cricket, like life, goes on regardless. Without characters — beings apart — it is but a faceless passage with scarcely a worthwhile memory. The competent plodder, the workmanlike side, admirable and necessary as they may be, leave us ultimately with no more than a line in Wisden. A hundred before lunch, on the other hand, is not quickly forgotten. "One crowded hour of glorious life is worth an age without a name." So too, the true measure of any era, is reckoned by those who adorn it.

The need for notable deeds and records may be taken as read. Granted the presence of superior talents, these will inevitably arise. The question of balance between bat and ball, however, is not nearly so clear, and is more likely to provoke controversy. I refer, of course, to the paying spectator; no doubt the players could reach a more or less standard verdict as to what determines a sporting wicket, and how best the laws be applied. One imagines, however, that the public tend rather to uphold the fashion of their youth, expecting, and feeling safe with, the familiar. Views will therefore vary from one generation to another.

The terribly slow pitches between the wars, for instance, taken in conjunction with the old L.B.W. ruling stacked the odds heavily against the bowlers. Yet if triple centuries and totals of 600 constituted your idea of entertainment, you did not shed too many tears. Equally, it could be said that the dust-bowls of the mid-fifties made batting something of a lottery, restricting the skills of the natural stroke-maker; but what Surrey supporter of that time would have complained that what virtually amounted to an England attack had conditions too much in its favour? So you see it *is* largely a matter of where your sympathies lie.

Nevertheless, the foregoing are hardly symptomatic of equal rights. How such uneven contests come about is perhaps not of major concern here, but while we are about it, a brief history of the game's ebbs and flows may do no harm.

As with all sports, cricket is evolutionary — subject to constant change in the face of each new contingency. Bowlers conceive fresh innovations; batsmen seek means with which to counter them; a ceaseless battle of wits ensues. Such is the natural order of things, without contrivance from ruling bodies. But as we know, when man takes a hand, he does not stop at half measures.

To be fair, though, those who administer the laws could claim to be victims of circumstance. They may in the past have lacked vision, and been inclined to over-react, but whatever misjudgments were made, were in response to public demand. Once interest in a sport becomes widespread — or 'box-office' as they call it — then to a large extent, popular opinion calls the tune. So with cricket. Here, one suspects, runs rather than wickets have formed the game's main appeal, and in consequence, wickets in the '90s were prepared accordingly. So far, so good. Pitches worthy of the calling, put cricket on a new plane — a move that heralded a classic era. Batsmen great by any standards found a fitting stage on which to display their talents; gates flourished accordingly. Victorian best promised value for money — none more so it would seem than the much-loved, bearded patriarch who reigned supreme. You could say, it was just what the Doctor ordered.

All eras pass, of course, and regrettably so, I sometimes think. Be that as it may, thirty years later a somewhat different picture had emerged. Batsmen still took the eye, but now rather too much. Occupying the crease became paramount. Obsessed with the notion that this was, in fact, what people wanted, it appears that a fundamentally sound assessment was carried too far. Over-prepared pitches were the unfortunate outcome. A flat-top of even bounce is one thing, a flat-top with no bounce, quite another. Lifeless wickets made for lifeless cricket. In all but wet conditions, or against rare types of bowling, runs were there for the taking, accumulated by anyone with sufficient patience. But runs made for their own sake often fail to excite.

The reader, of course, should not infer that a Hammond double-century drove one hot-foot to the beer tent; it is not standards, nor strengths as such, nor necessarily slow scoring we are discussing. Indeed, the late twenties and thirties are reckoned among England's strongest periods, and from that point of view, leave us with much that is memorable. Great players cannot of themselves be dull, nor fail to re-write the record books. We speak purely of the general tone of an age, and here all the signs were that, in the words of that same lordly Hammond, "Batting was too easy". Not just for him, which no doubt it was, but also for the ranks of lesser mortals. Were not the standing orders at Trent Bridge to, "Keep your wickets up lads, and the runs will come?"

Naturally, this decline was gradual rather than sudden, and not recognised until the bowlers begged for mercy. Likewise, until the emergence of a new generation with its revised L.B.W. law of 1937, together with more lively wickets, the imbalance remained. Then, as we saw, the advantage shifted too much the other way. The 60s bred a preponderance of seamers — not *quite* so prevalent today, I think — and for too long the game bore a stereotyped air. Once they could obtain a decision from a ball pitching outside off-stump and cutting back (where previously a batsman could escape even if plumb in front of all three!) bowlers who, pre-war, would have looked very ordinary, picked up wickets regularly — and economically. "Plug 'em down wide and let the ball do the rest" became their standard ploy, which com-bined with movement either way, was not only a sure remedy for success, but could also, at that pace, be accurately maintained. With, alas, far-reaching consequences.

Who now would employ spin, at least at both ends, with all its risks, when four such trundlers could alternate with one another throughout the day? The entertaining, though often wayward, leg-spinner became a luxury few could afford, and with rare exceptions, became obsolete. Even the more exacting figure-spinner was obliged to sacrifice 'bite', pushing the ball through more quickly and with less flight, and thus confirming the tendency to try to keep the batsmen quiet, rather than bowl them out. With a few glorious exceptions — one thinks of Emburey and Edmonds of Middlesex — this approach still prevails.

From this we must conclude that the right balance is an elusive quantity. In forcing matters, it seems, we have lost the means of fine control. The pendulum swings in too wide an arc, first one way, and then the other; whatever we try comes too late for instant reversal of well-ingrained trends. But let us look to the silver lining. It follows that in the course to to-ing and fro-ing, we must at times have touched a happy medium — the mid-shades of the spectrum that for us spell truly competitive cricket. Somewhere 'twixt evil extremes, lies the just balance we seek.

What, in principle, are the criteria for this? One can't be too rigid, of course, but ideally one wants a wicket that is true yet fast, which allows the ball to come on to the bat, and enables batsmen to play their strokes. At the same time, the resourceful bowler should always feel he is in with a chance, even against the best. One stresses, 'resourceful' for it is surely when runs or wickets come equally to artist and artisan, that their currency becomes devalued. Only master batsmen should appear to make run-scoring look easy; the worthy bowlers must yet take the wickets. Or what benefit their talents?

One aspect we have not mentioned is attitude — for which there can be no legislation. You can make bats the size of road shovels, or wickets a yard wide, but if the players themselves are not of a positive mind, no law on earth will effect a change. The mental approach remains one of life's intangibles, and is usually indicative of the particular age in which the individual lives. However, I do not propose to enlarge upon what is at best a generalisation, subject to all manner of provisos, and in itself far from conclusive. As always, we could find exceptions to the rule. Just as laws can never wholly suppress a great player's skills, so there will ever be those to whom negative tactics are pure anathema — and thank Heaven for them. Enough said.

With our analysis of guide-lines complete, we turn to personal persuasions. Given that these count for so much, how does one evaluate nostalgia? Our golden days, of course, are liable to be *over-romanticised*, but does that really matter? Eulogising the past has always been a trait of the human make-up, a weakness — if such it is — which applies to us all. Nothing will ever be quite what it once seemed to be. But it is high time we got down to business, which, if you need reminding, is to highlight such summers as come near to meeting our ideal, while perhaps rekindling a memory or two. If I presume the role of judge, then may one hope that you, the jury, will "find with me?" I rather feel you might. Over to the start of play.

II – The Fabulous '47

For all the vagaries of our climate, quite a number of summers pass muster. Yet in some of these, the cricket has by no means matched the weather. 1983 is an example. Of no season, however, was this less true than of one which will still be green, I fancy, in the minds of those with a half-century to their name. This was, of course, the fabulous season of 1947. Now, the stickler for perfection — and such he would have to be — might argue that here the bat had rather the better of things. This is fair comment, but only up to a point. Certainly, in a period of post-war rebuilding, few top-class bowlers remained, and fewer still were forthcoming, particularly of the quicker sort. Consequently, veteran Doug Wright and 'new find' Alec Bedser, both medium paced, were not only England's spearhead, but their stock bowlers as well, and, as such, were apt to be overworked. Bedser in particular suffered, and as a result was dropped after the second Test. Even so, the fact that he and sixteen others took over a hundred wickets (Tom Goddard 200) suggests that the bowler was not entirely at a discount.

At all events, it would be churlish — even sacrilege — to find fault with a summer that proved, among other good things, the annus mirabilis of the Terrible Twins, Compton and Edrich, whose phenomenal run-gathering may never be equalled. One might fill a chapter with the legendary deeds of that prolific pair, and better men have already done so, but our concern is less with a day-by-day account of their wondrous harvest, and more with the broad impressions that they made. Nevertheless, if one referred to 1947 simply as 'their year', few would be in doubt as to whom you referred. The Middlesex pair bestrode the summer like colossi.

Not that interest centred on those two alone. Even a brace of swallows does not make a summer. Elsewhere our cup ranneth over. Throughout the land, runs were scored at a merry rate, records were broken and attendances reached unprecedented levels. In addition, the visiting South Africans were not devoid of a world-class batsman or three. And all this under blue skies, from which a smiling sun blazed hotter as the days progressed. Yet pervading the cricket was something else besides — a spirit and an atmosphere the like of which we might never know again.

The carefree mood of a nation released from the shackles of war-time restraint is not, I think, easy to convey to younger readers, yet all who shared in that resurgence will readily concur. A public starved of authentic sport needed little wooing, and in fact would have settled for something less than the cornucopia that awaited us. Though 1946 had officially seen the resumption of the first-class game, the appalling weather and sad and inevitable gaps in the ranks, had conveyed an odd sense of unreality to the season. In twelves months, the transformation was complete.

Weeks of almost unbroken sunshine proved the ideal setting for men eager to parade talents laid fallow during six barren years. A season's reorientation now found them fully in tune with the needs of the day, whether consciously or not. It all seemed pre-ordained. Here people were seeking long overdue pleasure, armed only with goodwill and ready appreciation. That being so, the players proved more than equal to the task. And not purely as entertainers; one felt that they too, knew a deep sense of enjoyment. Distance, we know, lends enchantment, yet weren't these the 'happiest days of all our lives?' Unique, in my experience, was the warmth of fellow-feeling that abounded on all sides. There was a deep desire, spreading beyond the boundary's edge, to relate with those in the middle. We were of one mind — cricket folk bonded in a common quest; crowd and performers together were caught up in the euphoria of a rare moment in time. It was as if we knew, deep down, that it would not last; that soon the sterner business of life would intrude; that joy would not find the eternity it always seeks but would come to us as it invariably does — tinged with sadness at its impermanence. That summer seemed to say: "Come, the clouds have passed. You have survived a war — a free people in a green and pleasant land. I am here but briefly; indulge yourselves while you may." Which is exactly what we did.

So much so, in fact, that by August we risked being sated by the glut of runs and other rich offerings. But not quite. These were not your massive totals ground out at, perhaps, forty runs per hour. Around the counties, free-scoring was the order of the day. Leicestershire, for example, having made over 300 twice in the match, were entitled to feel safe from defeat. They lost to Middlesex by ten wickets. The latter's first innings of 637–4, left them needing 66 to win in just 25 minutes. In a bid for quick runs, Edrich and Compton went in first, while openers Robertson and Brown stood padded up behind the sight-screen in case a wicket should fall. It did not, of course, victory being achieved with five minutes to spare. That same Middlesex side — champions elect —

also ran up a score of 537–2 on a warmish day at the Oval. You can be sure that the Surrey bowlers found it so!

Needless to say, the chief contributors there were W. J. Edrich and D. C. S. Compton. During the summer, both men bettered Tom Hayward's 1906 record aggregate for a season of 3,518. Yet Edrich's tally of 3,539 (av. 80.43 including 12 hundreds) was all but over-shadowed in our pre-occupation with his partner's double coup. Denis Compton's 3,816 runs (av. 90.85) not only eclipsed the previous best by 300, but also included 18 centuries, thus passing Sir Jack Hobb's old record of 16. Compton's 73 wickets, in itself an achievement, seemed almost an anti-climax by comparison, yet, at inspired moments, he could turn a match with his unorthodox left-arm 'chinamen'.

In bowling, however, Bill Edrich had much the edge, though bare statistics tell only half the story. Until a shoulder injury in August effectively curtailed that side of his career, he had taken 67 wickets with some pretty ferocious fast bowling, and, in Bedser's absence, represented England's main strike force. A cricketer of immense heart, Edrich was only slightly less fluent than his most flamboyant partner. Indeed, in terms of value to both club and country, there was little to choose between them. One thinks the figures of either will take a good man to surpass. With so much less first-class cricket played today, they surely never will be.

Still, if they rode on a cloud of their own that summer, there were many who might have shone in less spectacular times. These we will come to; for the moment let us stay with that strong Middlesex side. Strong in batting, that is; the attack was something of a miscellany, though more than useful just the same. Only limitations, of course, are less exposed when you have hundreds of runs to play with — a luxury that was seldom lacking. The principle source of them we know about, but a team is a team, and more often than not the Twins were able to build on a solid start. Brown and Robertson were a sound, well-established opening pair, cast, as so often works well, in rather different moulds. While Sid Brown was your staunch, bread-and-butter county man, the stylish Jack Robertson fell only just short of the highest class, and was to gain an England cap before the season was out. Their true merit was seen when Test duty deprived the side of its big guns. Then, singly or together, they did much to ensure that Middlesex maintained their championship challenge. Their's could not have been an enviable role. With half the ground — including the present writer — impatient for them to make way for the main attraction, a lengthy stand was liable to meet with mixed reactions. Still, no one, I suppose, was too concerned if they got out. Pure conjecture on the contents of a vivid imagination, of course. I fancy that as good pros, such thoughts never entered their head.

No less daunting, one imagines, was the prospect of *following* the Lord's idols to the wicket. After a stand of, say, 200, in better than even time, this was no occasion for a grafter to play himself in. The momentum needed to be maintained, and here again they had just the right men for the job. Skipper Walter Robins — that evergreen cavalier — could not be other than enterprising. Always capable of something, with bat or ball, he not only made an ideal number five, but also contributed much to the county's success through his inspiring leadership. In Robins' absence — he missed none of the key games, though — George Mann proved an able deputy. George had something of his mentor's panache — so much a part of the old amateur tradition — and likewise was a lusty hitter of the ball in middle-order.

So the top four batsmen were followed by two others adept at hammering quick fifties. And the batting did not end there. Of those who could not command a regular place, Harry Sharp would have done so in many a county, Alec Thompson played at least one match-winning innings, while a newcomer, Alan Fairbairn (do you remember him?), got off to the best of starts by scoring a century in each of his first two county games. In fact, given their best side, they had scarcely a tail at all. Wicket-keeper Leslie Compton, who with brother Denis helped Arsenal win the F.A. Cup in 1950, could also bat usefully, while of the bowlers, senior-pro Jim Sims was a good man to have at number eight, Jack Young could hold up an end, and only paceman Laurie Gray might be termed a rabbit.

But just three bowlers? Well, we did hint that this area bordered on the unconventional, which meant that there were few who did not turn an arm. But that misleadingly, perhaps, suggests an array of 'bits and pieces' bowlers, called up only for a relieving stint. It was not so, of course. Of those not played as specialist bowlers, Edrich, as stated, took the new ball for England, and for three overs was as fast as anyone in the land. Lack of inches was well compensated by a high-leaping action, calculated to strike fear into the faint-hearted. He certainly would have unnerved me.

Compton too, although expensive, as bowlers of his type often are, more than once proved a match-winner. Similarly, Robins, both by trade and nature, was essentially an attacking bowler. A shrewd exponent of leg-breaks and googlies, he had developed his craft on dead, pre-war wickets, where spinners relied mainly on length and rainfall. One *had* to attack in order to trouble top-class batsmen, and this he had done to good effect. Now forty-one, he saw the captaincy as his first responsibility, and tended to bowl himself sparingly, nevertheless weighing in with some useful wickets.

There were others too, who came good from time-to-time, notably the schoolboy prodigy, Ian Bedford, who was sadly to die at the wicket, aged only thirty-six.* One consoles oneself with the thought that if such an end had to be, at least it was in some sense a fitting one. We might all do worse when the time comes, but that lies in other hands so let us direct our thoughts to more immediate matters.

Having established that the auxiliaries were more than make-weights, that they all took wickets, and some a good many, it was, of course, the case that the brunt of the donkey-work fell to the accredited bowlers. Of these, Laurie Gray, who shared the new ball with Edrich, was the classic unsung hero. Medium-fast, straight, he was prepared to bowl all day, though knowing few great ones. All sides have need of a stock-bowler such as he. Yet in those days, Middlesex, as did most other counties, looked more to the spinners for the bulk of their wickets. One way or another, they possessed one of almost every type. Some bought their wickets; others were expected to bowl their overs at reasonable cost, Jack Young and Jim Sims, usually doing so.

Young, slow left-arm, bowled tidily enough to finish fourth in the national averages, with 159 wickets av. 17.38, and thus earned selection for the fourth Test. His chance came late at the age of thirty-five, he being one of many whose best years were spent in activities having little to do with cricket. Sims was older still, although his leg-break bowling and sound batting had earned him several caps in the pre-war period. The wrist-spinner can never be truly economical, but this wily bird had acquired sufficient mastery of his craft to be kept on for long spells. A cunningly concealed googly trapped many a victim, and only Young of that side took more wickets. A hundred victims for a leg-spinner today would make front page news, but then, he and others, such as Eric Hollies, Titch Freeman and, in a faster style Doug Wright, performed the feat with unfailing regularity.

This, then, was the basis of the team which took the honours that year. Despite an ill-balanced attack when Edrich was unavailable, they were a well-equipped side, and worthy champions, though the drain of representative calls left them with little to spare over Gloucestershire,

---

*Ian Bedford's first-class career in fact but brief, he played much the better part of his cricket with Finchley, in whose service he died in 1966. He did, however, return to captain Middlesex through the 1961 and 1962 seasons.

the runners-up. These two had it much their own way, fighting it out between themselves for the best part of the season, yet their success derived from very different strengths.

Middlesex, as we have seen, relied on weight of runs speedily made, thus giving perhaps seven bowlers the maximum time in which to winkle out the opposition. Usually it was somebody's day. Conversely, Gloucester, although boasting batsmen of the calibre of George Emmett, Jack Crapp and the brilliant Charlie Barnett, were never a match for their rivals in this respect — who was? With few big totals to sustain them, they leaned heavily upon the spin combination of Tom Goddard and 'Sam' Cook, who, thoroughly at home on the famed Bristol 'turners' — among other places — continued to bowl sides out all season. Three hundred and twenty-six wickets between them in championship matches alone tells its own story.

Spinners, no less than pacemen, hunt better in pairs, and even more so when their strengths compliment each other. Here, Cook's orthodox left-arm turn, leaving the bat, provided the ideal foil for Goddard's sharply spun off-breaks. 'Long Tom' was now in his forty-seventh year, but had lost little to age. Ever aggressive, he loved to attack batsmen, seeking to *beat* them with every ball. He began as a fast bowler, and, whether because of the innate nature of that breed, or the years of toil on unresponsive pitches, had developed a positive hatred of those defending the stumps. But now the wheel had turned full circle and his 238 wickets — seventy more than anyone else that year — seemed to come as just revenge.

Cecil 'Sam' Cook, was a rather different proposition. The junior partner, by some twenty-one years, he had none of his mentor's hostile approach. A natural bowler, deceptive in flight, with a fine command of line and length, one felt he cherished the art of bowling for its own sake. 'Unlucky' to be selected for the first Test at Nottingham, he found the pitch so unhelpful, that in trying to extract turn he lost his control. Despite a career aggregate of 1,782 wickets, he was never picked again. For all that, he claimed 144 dismissals in the season, when these two so nearly bowled Gloucestershire to the championship.

No one else offered serious challenge — though this was mainly attributable to the unrelenting pace set by the leaders throughout.* Certainly most counties had their gifted individuals and colourful characters, each of whom left us with some piquant memory. Who, for

---

*To keep the record straight, both Middlesex and Gloucestershire, curiously, lost their very first championship matches, but from the time points tables appeared, these two, apart from a brief spell involving Derbyshire, were seen to occupy the leading places.

characters, each of whom left us with some piquant memory. Who, for instance, could fail to recall Joe Hardstaff, ever a crowd pleaser, not just to those in his native Nottingham, but to all who admired polished stroke-play. With every appearance of a Greek god, his batsmanship was of a mould befitting such a deity. If Hardstaff made runs — and over 2,000 flowed from his bat that year — he made them entertainingly. First capped by England in 1935, he had, by the time war intervened, established a place in what was by any standards a pretty formidable batting side. (In 'Hutton's Match' at the Oval in 1938, Hardstaff made 169 not out batting at number seven.) Sad to say, he could not quite recapture that form on the resumption after the war, flitting in and out of the Test side for a year or two, and then dropping out altogether. He was another one of those whose full powers were never realised.

J. C. Clay was also a man who impressed. Although nearing fifty and a Glamorgan player since 1921, this doyen of off-spin bowlers was still an integral member of a side destined to lift the championship the following year. To all intents in semi-retirement, he nevertheless played often enough and well enough to take second place in the bowling averages with 65 wickets at 16.44 apiece.* More remarkable still, in a season when batsmen were making hay, his overs were bowled at a cost of little more than two runs apiece. A master of flight and variation, John Clay was not only the finest bowler of his type the Principality has ever produced, but a warm personality too. The kindest of beings, good-humoured, of ready wit, his name will always remain corporate with Glamorgan cricket.

Who else? Worcestershire's Dick Howarth, of course, springs quickly to mind. He of the languid, cap-aslant air, this belying, perhaps, his intensity of purpose. Not even the lazy action of the slow left-armer leads one to think that wickets are come by without applied mental effort, and Howarth's haul of 164 was surpassed only by Goddard. Added to which, he was more than useful with the bat. In a career spanning twenty-five years, he numbers among the few who have taken 1,000 wickets and scored 10,000 runs. Still, he did find it rather droll, when late that summer, his form won him his first England cap at the ripe old age of thirty-eight.

No word of Yorkshiremen, so long the backbone, the true fibre of English sides. "When Yorkshire's strong, England's strong," was an oft heard cry. By their lofty standards, though, this represented a poor season, eighth place in the table being the lowest in living memory (how

---

*Effectively first place. G. W. Youngson of Scotland clinched the top spot by virtue of taking just 13 wickets at an average of 8.07. Clay thus headed all those with fifty or more.

times have changed!) The proud team of the thirties had largely grown old together, while others were lost to the war — Verity killed in action,* Bowes weakened by four years spent in prison camps. In 1946, the old guard assembled to take one more title, but now the county were faced with the necessity of rebuilding. Certainly, they did not want for a sound basis while they had Len Hutton, a technical master and England's number one by divine right. This was not perhaps *his* season, which was to come two years later, but even so, 2,500 runs spoke volumes for a man supposedly jaded after an exhausting tour of the Antipodes.

In peak form or not, there was no mistaking his pedigree. A Hutton out of touch did not embarrass you. Some players might play and miss for twenty minutes before ending their misery, but not 'Len o' Pudsey'. He could be pegged down, fail to pierce the field, yet he seldom 'struggled' and never ventured to hurry his shots — never, in fact, looked anything other than the textbook model he surely was.

Some measure of Hutton's class was revealed when serious injury threatened his career. An accident while in the services resulted in a shortened left forearm, a disability that might have greatly impaired the skills of a lesser man. Hutton made the adjustment with no discernible weakness. Some said that for a while he was vulnerable to the off-break, but from the boundary edge, nothing had changed. The perfectly-timed stroke play was still there. The famed, glorious cover-drive, unequalled in any age: the superb technique against the swing ball: all as before. Not least, the consummate ease of execution. Among contemporaries, he possibly played the quick men with more time than anyone.

It can only be speculation, but I often wonder if that challenge did not in fact, temper the fighting qualities so much in evidence in the onerous years ahead. You might say that anyone who mercilessly took 364 runs off Australia's best, did not want for application and hardly lacked the killer-instinct, but that is not quite what we mean. Hutton's dedication was never in doubt. At twenty he was hailed as a prodigy, and rightly so. At 22, he was an automatic choice for England, the world Test record his own. A star of an all-conquering county, his prospects shone bright.

The war rather changed things. He was now six years older, long out of match-practice, and like the rest of us, somewhat under-nourished. Never robust at the best of times, a long innings left him physically

---

*I think he died in an Italian prisoner-of-war camp (cf. also p.127).
cf. 'The War of the Roses': A. A. Thompson.

drained, and with all that, Hutton now had to come to terms with a handicap. By contrast, the 'old enemy', Australia, boasted one of her strongest-ever sides, possessed of a pace attack such as he could have rarely faced. Lindwall and Miller on pitches less placid than hitherto, were no sort of proposition for the faint-hearted. Then again, he was later to know the additional cares, and brickbats, that go with the England captaincy, moreover as the first professional to assume that particular mantle. Yes, Hutton needed to call on all his Yorkshire grit in order to fulfil with such distinction the dual role which was to earn him a knighthood. And as is often the case, might not adversity have served as a spur to achievement?

None of which, of course, has the slightest bearing on 1947, where perhaps the true explanation for Hutton not making the impact his figures might suggest, is to be found in his disappointing form in the early Tests. An uncharacteristic run of low scores, when set against the dazzling form of the Middlesex men, was bound to invite unfavourable comparison, particularly with Compton, who for so long in post-war years was Hutton's main rival as England's premiere batsman. He answered his critics in the best way possible — a faultless century on a turning wicket at Leeds, giving ever-constant Yorkshiremen much to cheer about. True class cannot be denied indefinitely.

Another survivor from Yorkshire's palmy days was no less than the current England captain, Norman Yardley. A neat if unspectacular batsman, and medium-pace change bowler, he had made his mark at Cambridge before entering the county side in the late 'thirties. Selected as vice-captain to Hammond on the ill-judged '46–47 Australian tour, he proved one of the few successes, and in the wake of the Gloucestershire man's prompt retirement, seemed the obvious choice for the leadership. Yardley was what one might call a 'good' cricketer — a natural games player, sound in all departments, but above all, a true sportsman, an amiable opponent and incurable optimist. Through no fault of his own, he was obliged, by and large, to skipper losing sides, both at county and national level, yet at all times he bore the cheerfully resigned air of one who accepts the inevitable. At any rate, Yorkshire saw fit to retain him in that role at a time when Hutton was captain of his country.

For the moment though, he was a winner. In this, his first full rubber, he led England to victory over South Africa without too many qualms. A saviour of causes rather than one to consolidate, Yardley's precious 99 at Trent Bridge offered a fine example of runs made when most needed. Such a score may be unlucky, but as John Arlott would say, it *is* memorable. As a bowler, he gave batsmen more to think about than an unimpressive action might suggest, and in Australia had earned something of a reputation as a partnership breaker. Surprisingly, in view of the selector's inability to find a settled attack, Yardley bowled over six overs in the entire series, yet here was a player always liable to pick up good wickets — as Bradman could testify three times over! No doubt the onus of leadership accounted for this decision, and as history tells us, winning captains make few mistakes! If perhaps not one of the resounding successes of 1947, Yardley's cordial disposition fitted well with the tone of that summer.

We cannot leave Yorkshire without mention of Bill Bowes. As remarked, his condition had greatley deteriorated during the war years, and in any case, thirty-nine was hardly the ideal age for a fast bowler to return to the fray. Yet that almost fanatical loyalty that Tykes display in Yorkshire's cause persuaded this great-hearted and unlikely sportsman to rally round once again. One says "Unlikely", because Bowes looked anything but an athlete. The tall, stooping frame, the bespectacled, rather serious face, spoke more of a scholar, and indeed, he was well qualified for the journalistic career that followed his playing days. Appearances, however can be deceptive. Though in the field, Bowes might have seemed lethargic, and often bore a disinterested air, his willingness to bowl all day was not in question. A shade short of genuinely fast, he operated off a run that, compared with the perambulations of many slower men today — would be adjudged economical. Even so, from his great height, he could extract both pace and bounce from all but the deadest wickets. In short, while capable of long spells the thirties so often demanded, he was still fast enough to force at least one wicket-keeper to take evasive action from a cartwheeling stump.

Bare figures do not always do justice to a player. You will not find in Wisden, for instance, that on a sweltering pre-war day at Scarborough, Bowes bowled almost unrelieved to take 9–121, when no one else could get the ball past the bat — a performance that he himself rates as probably his most satisfying. Something of that unflagging spirit was revealed when, at the war's end, a half-fit veteran bowled himself back into England contention. By 1947, however, Bowes realised his fast-bowling days were numbered, and made a decision to retire at the end of the season. He still easily topped the Yorkshire averages, and only four men bettered his figures nationally. Yorkshire might have slipped temporarily from grace, but with servants like Hutton, Yardley and Bowes to call upon, we felt that the White Rose would surely bloom again.

One could go on with recollections of those who played a part that summer, but I think we have fairly well covered the leading lights, or at least those whose contributions are best remembered. However, there is usually someone who finds a way into the record books on the strength of one isolated performance, and here was no exception. The moment of glory belonged to South African leg-spinner, V. I. Smith. His nine Test wickets at 48.77 runs each scarcely made him a candidate for the Bowler of the Year award. But a man's achievements do not always run true with the form book. In the tourists' match against Derbyshire in late July, Smith produced the startling figures of six wickets for one run off 4.5 overs. This, among other things, virtually ensured him top place in the tour averages. Every dog, as they say.

There was evidence too, that a new generation was on the way. As it happened, few of this budding crop went on to bigger things, but in the context of a single summer's highlights, that is quite incidental. We did not know that at the time, and saw them only as potential stars. Two, the Middlesex finds, Fairbairn and Bedford, have already received mention; both looked highly promising. Somewhat more meteoric, was the rise of Ken Cranston, the Lancashire amateur. Captain in his first season, he was selected for England after just two months in county cricket, and in the Leeds Test achieved great fame by taking four wickets for no runs in one momentous over. Heady stuff. Yet for one reason or another, within a year or so, all of these players had left the stage.

One prodigious newcomer who did go on to establish a county place, was the Surrey opener, David Fletcher. In a Whitsun run-spree on the Trent Bridge feather-bed (1,308 runs scored in the match) Fletcher, in only his second county game, made 194 out of Surrey's total of 701. Should that savour of easy pickings, 1,857 runs in his first full season betokened something more than a nine-day wonder. On the subject of Whitsun, by the way, it is worth recording that on the Holiday Monday, 20,000 attended the Roses match at Old Trafford, and 30,000 were at Lord's to watch Middlesex v. Sussex. And the championship race was barely under way. But what of the Tests, for many the yardstick of a memorable summer?

In that respect, it must be said that the series against South Africa was not a classic, though some excellent cricket was played by both teams. That aside, it somehow accorded perfectly with both our mood and needs. At that time, only Australia and South Africa were considered top-class opposition (that was to change three years later) but, as the recent Australian tour had shown, we clearly had not the bowling strength to trouble the likes of Bradman on firm wickets, nor sufficient batsmen of real Test class. Thus, a dour, backs-to-the-wall struggle would not have suited the sunny atmosphere of 1947; a crushing defeat might well have soured one's affection for it. (Few include the humiliation by the Australians in the following year among their cherished memories.) Here we needed a fillip: something to restore lost pride: a belief, that as in war, we were winners. Not least, we needed cricket of a kind to allow us to enjoy the summer to the full, to enable us to savour every moment of that rare spirit 'while we may'. Ideally then, our opponents should be first-class, and of comparable strength. Alan Melville's Springboks were made to order.

In fact, without help from the weather, it seemed unlikely that two top-heavy batting sides could bowl the other out twice. Not for the first time in cricket history, events proved us wrong. Although England, after early alarms, continued to make runs throughout, South Africa, who at one time looked certain to win the first, drawn, match, never again contrived to fire on all cylinders. Melville early on, and latterly Bruce Mitchell, were indeed difficult men to dislodge, but only Dudley Nourse showed any real consistency. Still, if a score-line of 3–0 to the home side suggests our visitors were outclassed, that exaggerated the disparity between, what on paper, were two well-matched sides.

Only an improbable last wicket stand of 51 by Hollies and Jack Martin — two men not renowned for their batting — prevented Melville's side from winning the first Test at Nottingham. At the Oval, in the other drawn match, they were in with a winning chance until the last hour. Individually, Melville began with three successive hundreds, which is not the worst example a captain can set his side; Mitchell played at least one historic innings, of which more will be said later and Nourse was, well — just Nourse, keen-eyed, quick to the pitch, ever looking to take the fight to the bowler, and seldom failing.

Of the bowlers, Athol Rowan, a world-class off-spinner, could be deemed unfortunate to encounter Compton in his best vein, but still posed problems whenever the ball turned. Likewise, Norman 'Tufty' Mann, slow left-arm, gave little away in the circumstances, as 127 maidens might indicate. True, of the faster men, only Lindsay Tuckett looked anything more than ordinary, but then England could not claim to be strong in this area, either. Again, both teams admitted to frailty in the middle order. So everything pointed to a close series, and in a normal season we might have had one. But Messrs. Edrich and Compton were not having a normal season, and there, simply, lay the difference.

It cannot be overstressed just how much England owed to these two. Compton's 753 runs, average 94.12, still remains a record in Anglo-South African Tests, and in the present climate, will stand for a long time.* Edrich, who in just four matches, scored 552 runs at an average of 110.40, was also the second highest wicket-taker with 16 at 23.12 apiece. Together, the two put on 370 for the third wicket at Lords (another record), 208 at Old Trafford, and 106 — out of 208 — in the first innings collapse at Trent Bridge. Only at Leeds, where England had only one innings, did either one or the other fail to make a hundred.

Yet even those statistics do not convey the true measure of their dominance, the proportion of runs that came from their bats, or the speed at which those runs were made. What, in June, had appeared to be a strong batting line-up, virtually ended at number four! Hutton, Washbrook, Edrich and Compton were as fine a quartet as you might find, but that said, there was, apart from useful contributions from such as Yardley and Evans, no front-line batting to follow. Indeed, England were to have trouble filling the number five spot for a good while. Significantly, of the seven centuries scored by Englishmen, the Middlesex pair made six of them. Twenty-one wickets between them was no bad effort either.

But it was as much the manner as the might of their achievements that carried the day. Tests at that time were over four days; a big total was of no tactical merit unless coming at a respectable rate. Edrich and Compton did rather better than that, the ball, which to them must have appeared like the proverbial football, channelling a well-worn path to the boundary. In keeping with a season that might have been stage-managed, they reserved their finest performance for Lord's and the second Test. An enthusiastic crowd of over 30,000 watched the first day's play, when Edrich (109) and Compton (110), both undefeated, put on 216 in 200 minutes, in spite of a half-hour's break for rain. Next morning we were treated to a brilliant display of strokes, orthodox and otherwise, as in a blistering onslaught, 136 runs came in the first session — with both batsmen still there.

Although Edrich left soon after lunch for 189, Compton went on at a giddy rate and, with Barnett, added 50 in twenty-five minutes before falling to a stinging catch with his score 208.

Again a huge crowd had had their money's worth; the local heroes had done them proud, and England were now in an impregnable

*South Africa last played official test cricket in 1969.

position from which victory came as a mere formality. But to underline the crucial extent to which these two predominated, we must consider that England, prior to Compton's dismissal, were 515–3, yet had slumped to 554–8 before Yardley declared. Thus between them, they contributed over two-thirds of England's runs; moreover, they got them at a speed which allowed two and a half days in which to bowl South Africa out twice.

In truth, it should be said that the overall run-rate of both sides would be considered headlong progress today, and while that may wax of lauding the past (an easy habit to slip into) one cannot help feeling that Test cricket has suffered as a result of a 'five day attitude'. In fairness, the timeless Tests of the thirties were equally responsible for slow play, but does this not all point to the fact that the clock adds an intriguing third dimension to the perennial unities of runs and wickets. However, that is an argument best pursued elsewhere, and we shall hasten back to wallow in those cavalier days of yesteryear.

Here the exception was Headingley, but then Yorkshiremen always did consider themselves to be different. On a pitch made sluggish by recent thunderstorms,* runs were never easy to make. So the stage was set for a new hero, the one man who, if not exactly revelling in such conditions, was surely the player best-equipped to use them to advantage. Hutton the incomparable, all season the poor relation, now came well and truly into his own, and where better for this lad from 'down t' road' to do so? He had yet to make a Test hundred on home territory, mainly because, strangely, he had never appeared there. Now, in every sense, was the time to remedy that unlikely omission; not just to reach the coveted landmark in front of a rapturous crowd — pleasure enough in itself — but to do so with an innings crucial to England's needs. And if it took five hours and a good deal out of him, the game was almost certainly won and lost through its making.

No one man wins a match, of course. Hutton was well supported by his old partner, Washbrook, and to a lesser degree, by Edrich and Yardley. Then again, someone had to bowl South Africa out, and this was readily accomplished through the game efforts of new cap Harold Butler, the Nottinghamshire fast bowler, Edrich, and, not least, Cranston, who wrapped things up with that memorable four-wicket over. For all that, only the most bigoted Southerner — and I am one (a

---

*In fact, 1947 was not quite the endless succession of sunny days we tend to imagine; rather, a summer that from cool beginnings, improved as it went along. August certainly, was hot, while it remained consistently fine right through until October. Which no doubt accounts for the impression of perpetual sunshine.

Southerner I mean) would deny that Hutton was the chief architect of a victory that clinched the rubber. In a match where South Africa, batting first, could not manage two hundred in either innings, Hutton reached three figures without giving a chance, being run out for exactly one hundred. This, on a wicket that was at no stage easy, and where for the only time in the series, Edrich and Compton struggled to pierce the field. A healthy first innings lead meant that England began their second requiring only 47 to win, of which Hutton made 32, a perfectly timed sweep to square-leg for six, bringing a fitting end to the proceedings. All Yorkshire basked in reflected glory, and even the ranks of Tuscany . . .

If the rubber was won at Leeds, the series by no means died there. In fact, in the sense that both sides were in contention until the end, the drawn game at the Oval proved the most absorbing of all. At Trent Bridge, after their first innings failure, England could only battle to save the game, and in so doing, left South Africa with little option but to bat out time. Lords, Old Trafford and Leeds all provided England with comfortable victories — twice by ten wickets — so while there was much scintillating cricket, none of the earlier matches had produced an exciting last day.

So easily might this fifth Test have bordered on an anti-climax. Three-nil up in the rubber, and winning the toss on a plumb, sun-baked wicket, a large total by England could well have killed off interest on the first day. While it is true that people will still flock to watch cricket even when there is nothing larger at stake, the match must be seen to have a purpose of its own if they are not to be left with a feeling that the players are merely going through the motions. In the normal way, of course, nothing is more guaranteed to gladden the hearts of home supporters than to watch their own batsmen taking the opposition apart. At Lord's and elsewhere, no Englishman complained that Edrich and Compton were ruining the game as a contest. But then the series was alive, and indeed at that time, England were fortunate not to be trailing. It is one thing to relish your side gaining ascendancy, another to delight in them ramming their superiority home, but rather a different matter when the issue is proved beyond doubt. Hammering opponents into the ground is not much fun and holds little appeal for most of us — and is this not a typically perverse English trait?

We like to win — who doesn't — but not I think, too easily. Moreover, we do not like to be *seen* to be trying too hard to win. We lack the killer instinct to trample foes into the dust; enough is enough; we begin to feel sorry, even embarrassed for them; we like to appear generous in victory — when we can afford to be so. It was much the same here. With the series won, and full satisfaction taken from the fact, our summer was complete. Few were anxious for England to make it four in a row. No one now would call for Yardley's head if they lost. The South Africans were decent fellows it seemed to be felt; — it would be nice if they were not sent home quite empty-handed.* What we wanted, to round the series off, was a good, competitive and highly entertaining match, happy in the knowledge that we could not now lose. The year 1947 did not often fail us.

Certainly no match in England has ever been played in such intense heat. 1921 had days as hot, possibly, as have had subsequent summers, likewise others since — but none surely was hotter than these four days of scorching sun, sweltering crowds, and fainting spectators, when no cloud, it seemed, would ever again cast a shadow, where a dazzling light tried the eyes and where a parched outfield, bleached yellow to near white, shimmered in the heat haze. High summer indeed! At times even the players wilted; South Africa's bowlers, particularly, unused as they were to the endless pounding of six-day-a-week cricket, often looked weary in their approach. One South African seemingly unaffected by the conditions, was Bruce Mitchell, and perhaps it is both right and fitting to dedicate the last echoes of the series to a visitor. For notwithstanding a display of pure genius by Compton, the batting of Nourse and Hutton, and other worthy contributions, this was surely 'Mitchell's Match'. But to do justice to the immensity of his performance, one must further stress the unpromising circumstances in which he laboured.

Needless to say, this was a good toss to win, and Yardley had no hesitation in batting. Thus, South Africa were put at an immediate disadvantage, not least, psychologically. Already well-beaten, they now faced an uphill task from the outset. Though the well-watered square was in much better shape than the outfield, a wicket baked rock-hard by day-long sunshine, promised runs for the taking. With Compton enjoying a bumper August, and Hutton running into form, a total in excess of 500, even without the injured Edrich, looked very possible. In that heat, the fielding side did not have a cheering prospect.

In the circumstances, however, they could be said to have got off lightly. Though Hutton made an elegant 83, several others, including Compton, got out when well set, and only a wag from the lengthy tail enabled England to reach 427. This was a safe enough, but by no means

---

*I don't know if the players felt that way, however, as stated, these are purely a spectator's impressions.

decisive score. Enter Bruce Mitchell, an opener of the highest quality, and at that time, the scorer of most runs in South Africa's Test history. Perhaps because of his sureness in defence, and his familiarity with the role of sheet-anchor, it is easy to think of him as a rather dour, imperturbable run-machine. That, however, gives only half the picture. The grace in Mitchell's attacking strokes belied the power with which, at times, he fairly thumped the ball through the off-side field, while he could always change his strategy to suit the needs of the side. A complete batsman, one might say.

There was no doubting his intentions here though. This was no time for heroics. England had virtually insured themselves against defeat; South Africa, it seemed, were committed to batting out a draw, as the best they might hope for. If this were to be achieved, long, patient hours at the crease lay ahead. Mitchell saw it as his first duty to consolidate and shore up one end while the innings took shape around him. To respond to a score of 400 in a defensive position is never easy; the immediate priority was to ensure that England batted again. With little reliable batting after Melville — who had dropped himself down to five — a lot rested on Mitchell's shoulders.

This was confirmed as he watched three wickets go down cheaply at the other end, during which time, Dick Howarth joined the select band of those who have taken a wicket with their first ball in Test cricket. 78–3. A stand of 86 with Melville helped retrieve the situation, after which he and Dawson saw them to 211 for 4 at the close of the second day, Mitchell 92 not out.

Next morning, as the last of the recognised batsmen, these two applied themselves to the task of avoiding the follow-on. Mitchell's hundred came with the inevitability of Christmas, while Dawson pushed steadily along before falling to Wright's googly. 243–5. Two wickets then fell quickly, which meant that with seven wickets down, South Africa still required 24 to avoid the follow-on. This was duly achieved, but when, quite surprisingly, Mitchell left soon after, the innings was not long in folding. South Africa were all out for 302, Mitchell 120. The England lead was 125.

★   ★   ★   ★   ★   ★

At this stage, you might well imagine that with just over ten hours remaining, the game but mid-way through and the wicket as good as ever, that, short of unforeseeable disaster, it was simply a matter of playing out time. Or at any rate, that only England might reach a winning position. In 1947, however, all things were possible, which gives one another good reason for writing about it, and, quite apart from the pure entertainment, the match as a contest was in no sense dead. Not while there was Compton (though to bowlers he was, I suppose, an all-too *foreseeable* disaster). Nor yet while one had Yardley at the helm, who with the series won, could so easily have played it safe, but was not made that way. Nor, indeed, while there was Mitchell — but we anticipate . . .

★ ★ ★ ★ ★ ★

England began their second innings just before lunch on the third day. Hutton and Washbrook went quietly along to the interval, but thereafter, under instructions to hoist the run-rate, moved briskly to 73 before both left in quick succession. Without Edrich to take command, Yardley's tactical plans were further thwarted in that new cap Jack Robertson, understandably anxious not to fail for the second time in the match, could not maintain the desired tempo. However, with Compton playing easily from the moment he came in, his partner's inability to force the pace, mattered less than it might have done. The captain seemed content to let Robertson jog along in support. Soon, had he known, few would be giving thought to Robertson at all.

Too often that summer, one was tempted to declare this or that Compton innings to be the best, but for sheer virtuosity — genius in flagrant mood — the feast he provided that afternoon would he hard to equal. Here was the man personified; or rather the perennial schoolboy with mischief aforethought; the gay improvisor, who as if wearied by the orthodox, indulged in every kind of rich extravagance. One moment cutting while yards down the wicket, the next, producing a cover-drive that defied the textbooks, but bisected the field just the same, then again, the casual one-handed sweep to long leg. All played with a bat as crooked as original sin, yet every shot middled. He had time, also, to change his mind in mid-stroke, and more than once had the slips anticipating an edged cut, only to drive handsomely to the long-off boundary. It was the old story of a man who, well in, was finding it difficult to get out.

He reached fifty in an hour, and while runs were always there for the patient, scoring quickly against a top-class spin attack on a now slowly turning wicket, was quite another matter. This was borne out by Robertson, Yardley and Cranston all meanwhile having perished in the attempt. Now, at 180–5, Howarth joined Compton, who unmindful of the traumas at the other end, grew bolder still, and in forty minutes of glorious, unrestrained impudence, raced merrily on past his hundred, before edging a cross-batted drive to Nourse at slip. 267–6, last man 113 — his runs coming out of 178 scored while he was at the wicket. The hero gone, I think we all felt a sense of personal loss, as for an hour and a half, Denis Compton had taken everyone on the ground along with him.

But Howarth, who later said he felt embarrassed at taking strike with Compton in such irresistable form, now made some lusty hits of his own, and with Evans joining in the fun, Yardley was able to declare the innings closed at 5.45 with the score 325–6. The runs had come in just 200 minutes. South Africa thus required 451 to win, with seven hours remaining,* a striking rate of 65 an hour — not impossible, of course, but still a tremendously tough assignment over so long a period. And even more so with only four front-line batsmen, one of whom, Viljoen, had yet to show any real form in the Tests. Yet Yardley, acting in good spirit, had striven to make a game of it and his challenge, by Test match standards, was a fair one. It would indeed have been surprising if Melville, with little to lose, had not decided to give it a go. On a still perfect wicket, he, Nourse and Mitchell were all capable of a long score, and, if they materialised, they might yet salvage a little consolation from the series.

In assessing their chances, however, it was not fair to argue that England's runs had come at close on 100 an hour. That was virtually the work of one man, and he riding a purple patch such as few could hope to emulate. No, South Africa's innings would need to be paced, a solid start providing a platform from which to mount a later offensive. At least two batsmen would have to make hundreds while, at the same time, leaving themselves the option to close up the game if things went wrong. It required someone to hold firm at one end, take charge of the innings, and if necessary adjust his game to meet the needs of the side. That man was Bruce Mitchell.

Clearly his first job was to try to ensure that South Africa entered the final day with all wickets in hand. At the best of times, weathering a half hour or so before the close puts one on a hiding to nothing. There is insufficient time to achieve anything substantial, yet time enough to lose valuable wickets. There is no time to succeed; there is plenty in which to fail. The bowlers are fresh, and able to operate flat out; the batsman, by comparison, is tired from a long day's exertions in the field. A lapse in concentration could well prove fatal. It is not a period

*These were six-and-a-half hour days — 11.00 until 6.30.

batsmen relish.

Mitchell had to face all these circumstances, and more. He was thirty-eight, and had spent not one, but the best part of three days in the field. The England bowlers, on the other hand, had not left the pavilion. Added to which, in Dyer, he had a new and relatively inexperienced partner, who would have to be shielded from the strike. Runs then, were of no consideration; survival was the watchword. With just two minutes remaining, however, Dyer fell prey to Wright's googly, the only consolation being that there was insufficient time for a new batsman to come to the wicket. That which South Africa wished most to avoid, had happened. 8–1. The balance had swung England's way.

★ ★ ★ ★ ★ ★

Runs, wickets, time: the dramatic unities of cricket: all were here. Batsmen against the clock — plainly the compelling feature of what promised to be a fascinating last day's play. 443 runs needed in six-and-a-half hours: nine wickets in hand: an asking rate of almost seventy an hour. Such equations would govern play to the end. It was strange then, that a climax rich in possibilities should attract a crowd of only 10,000, the lowest of the four days. This tends to substantiate our earlier point, that to many the finish is of secondary importance. Whatever deterred them, however, it was not the weather. Those who came, did so in summer best — the Oval a ring of bright colour amidst the drab urban setting. Those who came were not bad judges.

Eleven a.m. The time when conjecture would be put to the test. If England held the edge, it was a fine one. True, they had made the early break-through, yet that was not the scalp they most wanted. The quarry in question, endowed with hour-long powers of concentration, now set about wearing down the bowling, while Viljoen took such runs as he could before Wright attacked. The Kent man had plagued him all through the series, and, almost as soon as he came on, had Viljoen stretching forward to be comfortably stumped by Evans. 48–2. Last man 33. Mitchell, meanwhile, had reached 9 not out.

Nourse came in with much depending on him. Well behind the clock, South Africa would have to press on swiftly if they still entertained hopes of winning the match. In fact, Nourse immediately hit two crisp boundaries, indicating that he, at least, was bent on going for a win.

He appeared to see the ball well from the start, and continued to prosper, finding the gaps with those punchy, well-timed strokes that were so much his trademark. The chase began; slowly the innings gained momentum. Then, attempting a late cut off Howarth, Nourse got a bottom edge that flew straight into Hutton's hand at slip — and out again. Ten thousand simultaneous gasps of disappointment told of its significance. South Africa breathed again.

When a batsman is dropped, one of two things usually happens. Either he heeds the warning, and steadies down, or decides to ride his luck. Nourse chose or was impelled to choose the latter, immediately taking fourteen off the luckless Compton's first over, and sixteen from his next two — which promptly saw yesterday's hero banished to the long field. Cricket, the great leveller.

South Africa lunched with their score 147–2. Nourse was 63 — made in 80 minutes, Mitchell 41. 304 were needed in four hours — 76 an hour. Mitchell had only 37 runs to show for his morning's work, yet had never remotely looked like getting out. Unglamorous maybe, but highly effective and precisely the innings Melville required of him at this stage.

The afternoon brought about a change of tactics, however. Thirsting for a wicket, Yardley elected to take the new ball as soon as it became due, which in those conditions was always likely to prove a double-edged sword. While there was precious little movement for the bowlers, the harder ball now came faster off the bat, allowing both batsmen to profit from the close-set field. Then again, medium-fast bowling to a veteran opener, there since the start, came much like cherry cake to Billy Bunter. South Africa saw this as their moment of opportunity. Not since Trent Bridge had they been in a position to win a Test; the next hour or so was make or break time, the outcome of this partnership, crucial.

They put on 80 in the first hour, with Mitchell, making a fine sense of occasion, discovering the strokes with which to outpace his partner, 40 to 34. Breaking out of a defensive groove is never easy, yet he launched into attack in mid-over, as if suddenly deciding that the time was now ripe. Yardley, desperate for a break-through, and getting no joy from his quick men, called back his spinners. Now came one of those bizarre incidents on which matches so often turn. Nourse was three runs short of his hundred, when he stepped across to allow a ball from Howarth to pass harmlessly down the leg side. It seemed to brush his pad, however, and Howarth asked for l.b.w. 'Not out'. Evans, who also heard the click, now appealed for a catch behind. 'Not out'. Just then, Jack Robertson at square leg, shouted: "It bowled him," and pointed to a bail lying beside the stumps. Jack Smart, the square-leg umpire had also seen it fall, and, adjudged out at the third time of asking, poor Nourse had to go. He had surely deserved a century, but thanks to him, his team at 232–3, were now on course to win.

Nevertheless, the break-up of a long partnership of 185 priceless runs was bound to disrupt the tempo and even more so when the next man to the wicket bore the dual responsibilities of captain and last specialist batsman. How South Africa must have regretted not having a number six capable of a punishing innings. As it was, they had two men who might make 40 or 50, while the tail, dare one say, was the same one that had capitulated in just six balls at Leeds. Still, conditions there had been rather different. It was to be hoped they would acquit themselves somewhat better on this friendly strip.

For the moment, though, Melville was under no great pressure to hurry things along, and it was not in his side's best interests that he should do so. With Mitchell well entrenched and keeping the score-board ticking over, ten minutes spent playing himself in seemed a sounder long-term investment. This he proceeded to do, content to present a broad bat to anything straight, though looking to score off the loose delivery. It was thus all the more galling when, just as he appeared to be settling in, he was caught behind off Cranston, from a purely defensive push. 247–4. In the space of fifteen minutes South Africa's fortunes had changed dramatically, but with six wickets still in hand, a win could not yet be discounted. Not, at least, while Mitchell remained.

Dawson came out to join him with orders to go for quick runs, showing that Melville had not abandoned the chase, but immediately square-cut Cranston into Howarth's hands at gully. Fullerton was next to take up the fight, and played several crisp scoring strokes before, like Melville, he edged a catch to Evans behind the wicket. 266–6. The time now, five minutes to four. South Africa wanted 185 to win in 135 minutes. Their chance was surely gone. Indeed, with the tail exposed, saving the match might be no easy matter. Not for the first time, the middle batting had let them down badly, four wickets going down for just 34 runs. Who spoke of 'cricket's glorious uncertainy'?

Little seemed more certain, however, than that Mitchell would reach his second century of the match. This he achieved with two firmly struck fours off Howarth, almost before the new batsman Mann, had found his bearings. That it was made at twenty runs an hour scarcely detracted from its worth. The man who could least afford to get out had, in five hours at the crease, never once looked like doing so. Nor could he yet rest content. Over two hours still remained, and a vulnerable tail would need protecting from the strike. Yardley, at last in a position of tactical strength, could crowd the bat with little fear of counter attack; the day was still unbelievably hot. Anyone's concentration might lapse in these circumstances.

After tea, Mitchell continued to take such runs as were offered, while Mann, attempting little more ambitious than a forward push, stayed gamely for half an hour before snicking Wright to short leg. Five o'clock — three wickets to fall. The crowd, silent, absorbed as it had been all day in the fascinating see-saw of events, now sensed an England victory. Tuckett, next to come in, might give useful support, but no one else could really be expected to resist for long.

This was indeed a torrid time for South Africa. Yardley could not only afford to keep men clustered round the bat, but could also claim another new ball, one which would pose a very different threat from the one which was shown such scant respect earlier. Having a number nine at one end always gave hope of a break-through, while even Mitchell at last showed himself fallible, edging Wright's leg-break to Evans, who, of all people, dropped it. That apart, they weathered the storm safely enough, and with the new ball out of the way, entered the last hour 111 behind England. Runs now, of course, were of purely academic interest, yet England came no closer to clinching victory either. No further chance was given, and in fact, during the last half hour the batsmen took some easy runs off the 'friendly' bowlers, to reach 423–7 at the close, Mitchell 189 not out. Just 27 runs separated the two sides.

Of course, once South Africa's middle batting had crumbled, England were in no danger of defeat and Yardley could always have spread the field if a serious onslaught had threatened. But one was still left to ponder what might have happened had Mitchell received the support he was entitled to expect. That five batsmen made only 57 between them, lays further emphasis on the immensity of his contribution. 309 runs for once out amounted to almost half South Africa's match aggregate. He was on the field for all but fifteen minutes. Some measure of his concentration was illustrated — so the story goes — in the final period, when half-an-hour after Mann was out, Mitchell set off for a run, but seeing the ball reach the boundary, pulled up in mid-pitch to come face to face with Tuckett. "Lindsay?" blinked Mitchell in surprise. "When did Tufty go?"

So a match that could have gone either way, ended with honours even, and one felt that in a game played in such excellent spirit, this was the fairest result. All one had hoped for and more, had been granted.

After eight years, Test cricket was back with us as an integral part of the summer. If there were glaring weaknesses in the England side, weaknesses that were to be cruelly exposed a year later, then we conveniently chose to ignore them. Today was all that mattered, and today we had won — and also been richly entertained.

Before we leave the Test arena, we can see how that final match contained those contrasting elements of light and shade that are such a part of cricket's charm. The performances of the two central characters, Mitchell and Compton, were as different as chalk and cheese — and one might safely say that given a choice of one or the other, most would plump for the cheese. But leaving aside the fact that even Compton could not turn on that kind of display to order, would we have valued it so highly had he been able to? Like diamonds, the worth of such an innings lies in its rarity, and whatever we may think, a plethora of runs, day in, day out, would ultimately be little better than endless stone-walling. Christmas all the year round is not really Christmas; one needs the contrast of a solid backcloth to set off the bright jewels.

Should that suggest that the Mitchells of this world are no more than warm-up acts for the top performers — the shadow in the spectrum as it were — this is, of course, not so. In their rightful place, it is possible to enjoy both equally — just as one might relish roast beef and strawberries and cream, though not on the same plate. Indeed, the meaty flavour of a tense rear-guard action, such as we saw at the Oval, is every bit as enthralling as a whirlwind hundred. Without doubt, a balanced diet is necessary for good digestion.

The one disturbing feature of that Oval Test, was that because of some evil quirk of the fixture list, it coincided with the crucial championship match between Gloucestershire and Middlesex, a game that virtually decided the destination of the title. Many a patriot sat with one ear cocked for news from Cheltenham. In the event, Middlesex won a low scoring match by the comfortable margin of 68 runs. In a fixture which might have been billed 'Bowlers v. Batsmen', it was perhaps surprising that Gloucestershire did not do better on their own notorious 'turner'. And all the more so when the 'batsmen' were greatly weakened by the absence of Compton and Robertson, while injury cost them the services of Edrich as a bowler. Certainly the West Countrymen bowled well enough, particularly Goddard, who had the remarkable figures of 15–156, but not the first time that summer, it was their batting that let them down.

In fact, Edrich's first innings 50 proved the highest score of the match, and this, together with more fine spin-bowling from Young (9 for 82) and Sims (8 for 89), did most to see Middlesex home. It gives some idea of the state of the pitch, that the three pace bowlers sent down only 15 overs between them, and claimed just one of the 40 wickets to fall. There were not too many drawn games at Cheltenham.

The Test series was over, the Championship won, but still the summer went on and on. September's heat suffered little by comparison, and the festival matches were played out in day after day of endless sunshine. At Hastings, a strong South of England XI met the South Africans in their farewell fixture — a match the visitors were very keen to win, as they made clear by batting on to 510–8 declared in the first innings. Rowan and Mann bowled tidily enough to dismiss the South for 341, but, like others before them, were powerless to stop Compton racing to 101 at a run a minute — his seventeenth hundred of the season — and one that took him past Sir Jack Hobbs' record. The South Africans went on to win fairly comfortably, but how they must have been sick of the sight of Compton that summer.

And so to the final encounter, and now defunct Champion County v. The Rest fixture, which took place at the Oval on 13th September, over four days. As a post-script to the season, the icing on the cake, no writer of fiction could have conceived a more suitable epitaph; in almost every sense, this match reflected the whole story of the summer. That most regular of spectators, the sun, attended on all four days. Equally predictably, Middlesex won the toss and batted, but the script took a wrong turn when they plummeted to 53–3. Need I say what happened next? A match or two earlier, Compton had received the first intimation of the knee trouble that was to plague, and eventually curtail, his career. Now, leg heavily strapped, the man who was still to win an F.A. Cup medal, hobbled out to join his partner-in-crime in a well-rehearsed double act.

Alec Bedser, with something to prove, had already dismissed both openers for a mere seven runs; he was to wait a good while for his next success. In fact, the bowlers only respite that day came 138 runs later, when Compton had to leave the field for further treatment. The two were still together on Monday morning and looked as permanent as the surrounding gasometers until Edrich was stumped off Goddard for 180. The Rest's suffering were nowhere near done; they could not set a field for Compton, and one doubts if he could have got out had he tried. In fact, he perpetrated what was probably one of the most remarkable strokes ever.

Going down the wicket to Goddard, his feet locked together, causing him to fall forward on to the damaged knee. It was the quintessence of Compton that summer, that, as he fell, he stroked the ball sweetly through mid-wicket for four. No wonder bowlers came to believe that he could not be bowled to. Goddard did have his revenge a little later, when Compton was also stumped — by which time he had cavorted his way to 246, with 30 fours. What a pity he was not fully fit! Together the redoubtable pair had scored 426 out of a total of 543-9 declared. This, off an attack comprising Bedser, Butler, Wright, Howarth and Goddard.

What followed was again an old familiar tale. The Middlesex bowlers, with a big total behind them, had time to work their way twice through the opposition, leaving a rightful champion county needing just 21 to win. This was achieved early on the fourth day, Edrich, perhaps significantly, making the winning hit. Those were the days.

And there it all ended. As then, one is reluctant to bid farewell to that eternal summer, yet leave it we must, for other seasons with other heroes await our pleasure. Much has been left unsaid, of course, but it was never the intention to offer more than a kaleidoscopic view of events as seen through the eyes of one who — like you perhaps — took his place in the 'free seats' along with the rest. The 'free seats' at Lord's. Indeed a fond memory.

No doubt we each have our own favourite memories of 1947, but for a Harrow lad such as I (the town, not the school) Lord's was the place to be. With Middlesex always 400-8 declared — the Twins a hundred apiece — and two opposition wickets in the bag — what more could one ask of a warm, cloudless Saturday? Perhaps it was not *quite* like that, but that's how it appeared, and impressions count for a good deal. So far as I am concerned, just as it never rained during childhood summer holidays, so it never — well hardly ever — dampened our enjoyment at Headquarters.

In those days too, before towering office blocks poked obtrusive noses over the wall, to stroll around the the perimeter was to know tranquility. Passing the Grace Gates; on, behind ivy-covered sanctums, steeped in cricket history, catching a worm's-eye view of play from beneath the stand. All made it hard to believe one was in N.W.8. I could be biased, of course, but how many, with hand on heart, can claim to be wholly impartial in matters of sport? At this distance, I have no doubt that others derived no less pleasure at Maidstone or Melton-Mowbray, Headingley or Hove. It is not the venue that counts, but the cricket played there.

And what cricket it was. And will we ever know anything quite like it again? For sure there will be fine summers, great players, just as there always have been. Nevertheless, I fancy that the next time two batsmen account for 7,000 of the season's runs, I shall no longer be of this world, but shall be basking on some green Elysian field, in, of course, endless sunshine. One does not need to be a cricket-lover to recall a golden summer, but if willow's sweet click hastens your steps near the County Ground, then 1947 offered a double bonus. Everyone knew who 'they' were.

III – Super Statistics

We move further back now, to the period between the wars, where the summers, if not quite faithful to the image that lingers with us, were in fact, generally more consistent than those of post-war days. Two in particular, 1921 and 1929, were of a kind for which weather men like to take credit, though, for entirely different reasons, neither can be included in our digressions. 1929 was notable for the visit of 'Nummy' Deane's South African side, but that apart, was singularly lacking in happenings of great moment; 1921, on the other hand, contained rather too many of the wrong variety. Did not, among other things, an Australian captain contrive to bowl two consecutive overs?*

That seems to have been Warwick Armstrong's only mistake that summer. His fabled side steam-rollered their way through the tour undefeated, an overwhelming 3–0 victory in the Tests being almost taken for granted. By odd coincidence, England's fortunes against the old foe followed a near identical pattern in each of the post-war periods. Both times, a depleted Old Country encountered exceptionally strong opposition — indeed, argument continues as to which of these great sides was Australia's best ever. Both times England went through two series — home and away — without winning a single Test. Both times there followed — 4 defeats in Australia, though the score-line failed to do us justice. And both times — and this defies credibility — the tide was turned, when in 1926 and 1953, after four drawn games, England triumphed at the Oval. And they say lightening never strikes in the same place twice! Still, if it was remarkable that the two sequences should bear such close similarity, the fact that a battle-weary nation takes time to regain its feet gives somewhat less cause for wonderment.

Very little good comes out of a world war, and while cricket's welfare might be of small consideration, it is affected like anything else. 1914 marked the end of an era, and for many, a golden one; even when fully recovered, cricket could never be the same game again. Here were the

---

*The incident took place at Manchester, where Armstrong, a somewhat controversial figure, came in for some barracking from the crowd. At the end of his over he refused to continue until the noise subsided, and bade his team sit down on the field. After several more outbursts, the game restarted, when in the confusion, Armstrong proceeded to bowl the next over, thus making two in a row. How this went unchecked is hard to imagine, but at 22 stone, he was perhaps a man one didn't argue with.

first signs that the days of amateur dominion were coming to an end; a second such holocaust was to further hasten the move towards equality. Again much more so than in the last post-war period, the twenties were cloaked in a grey austerity, where dole queues became an accepted way of life (rather as now, I fear). Not least, sadly, able young men were in short supply.

Deprived of continuity, the life's blood of all sport, the cricket of 1919 was less than satisfactory. A year later, a 5–0 drubbing in Australia confirmed the low state of our game, and Armstrong's return visit did nothing to lift English morale. Defeat in eight consecutive Tests — a sequence without parallel — led to desperate measures. No fewer than 37 players were tried in a bid to find a counter. The one man who might have made all the difference, Jack Hobbs, played in just one Test before appendicitis put him out for the rest of the summer. These were not exactly times you told your young about. Thus, though arguably the hottest year of the century, 1921 was not a season to warm English hearts.

But all things pass, and by 1926 the ashes were back in safe keeping. This saw the start of one of England's strongest eras, where one feels that only the advent of Bradman stood between us and long-term dominance. In those days, however, it was more often than not the domestic scene that took precedence; so on the established premise that one seldom finds total perfection, the next year to warrant appraisal is not best remembered for its Test series.

In fact, in more ways than one, it might be argued that 1928 fell short of the ideal, but surely a season that proved a statistician's delight can on no account be ignored. For those interested in keeping records of unique occurrences and feats both rare and wonderful, there has never been anything like it. If the bowler had generally the worst of things, the novelty of heavy scoring that was to prejudice the thirties, had not yet worn thin; if the summer's heat could not compare with the best years, there was sunshine enough. Sunshine enough, shall we say, for five batsmen to score over 3,000 runs — an event without precedent, and of course, unlikely to be repeated under the present-day structure. Even so, the fact that only nineteen players in all have achieved this feat and that 1947 was the last time it was twice recorded, ensures 1928 a place in cricketing history.

It gives some indication of the strength-in-depth at this time, that one of the quintet, Frank Woolley, was not considered for the forthcoming tour of Australia — a decision which sent up a wail of protest the length and breadth of England — while of the others, Phil Mead played in just one Test and Ernest Tyldesley three. Only Herbert Sutcliffe and 'Patsy' Hendren, who incidentally both managed the feat three times in their careers, could feel secure of their place. What's more, none of the five came higher than third in this season's averages, top honours going to Jardine and Hobbs, who averaged over eighty. It was, most definitely, not an easy time to break into the England side.

Again, another player that they could afford to pass over, Charlie Hallows, gave early warning of what was to come by achieving that cricketing nicety, 1,000 runs in May. This is rare enough in any case, but here was made all the more unusual by the manner of accomplishment. Coming to his last possible innings, Hallows was still 232 short of the mark. He made, as you might guess, no more nor less than 232 — and on the last day of the month as well, which again showed a nice touch of showmanship. Whether this came about by accident, or if some sense of arithmetical neatness prompted him to get out at that juncture, we cannot say, but whichever the case, he remains the only man who could accurately claim to have made 1,000 runs in May!

All this might argue for a batsman's paradise, which no doubt it was, but one bowler, at least, had no cause to complain of the wickets that summer — A. P. 'Titch' Freeman. The Kent leg-spinner indeed went some way to redressing the balance, by taking no fewer than 304 wickets — another record — and while we know that records are there to be broken, this one is surely destined to stand for all time. It also marked the beginnings of yet another feat without parallel, one also likely to remain so. In the eight seasons from 1928–35, Freeman never once took less than 200 wickets, taking more than 250 in six of them, and reaping an awesome crop of 2,090 victims. No one came closer to equalling his 304 wickets than he himself.

It was strange then, that a bowler who for eight years was the most prolific wicket-taker in the land, should play in only six Tests in that time, and just 12 in all. It could hardly be that his county record owed everything to local or helpful pitches, different from those he would find at Test level. Wickets at this time were more or less uniform, and in any case, as a leg-break and googly merchant, Freeman was not dependent on grassy turners for success. In addition, Grimmet and O'Reilly, both similar in type, were Australia's outstanding bowlers in this period.

Nor can it be claimed that, with Kent, he relied overmuch on a wicket-keeper who could read him for a good number of his victims. The man wearing the gloves for England and Kent was one and the same — Leslie Ames. One can only suppose that like others before him, Freeman lacked the Test match temperament — that he was a familiar, if extreme, case of the player with all the credentials at county level, who yet fails to do himself justice on the big occasion.

Mention of Ames brings us conveniently to the next supreme feat. In a year when all-time records fell to batsmen and bowlers, fieldsmen were not to be denied either. Ames, for one, touched new heights among wicket-keepers by assisting in the dismissal of 121 batsmen, though this was one record destined to last but a short time. Twelve months later, the same player bettered his own haul by six. However, one part of the record that neither he nor anyone else has improved upon was the number of stumpings — 52, most of them, of course, off Freeman's bowling. Between whiles, Ames, who could have been played for his batting alone, also found time to score nearly 2,000 runs. It is interesting to note though, that even had Ames been absent, his great contemporary and rival for the England spot, George Duckworth, would still have equalled the old wicket-keeper's record of 107 victims. One way or another, you could not keep the feats of 1928 out of Wisden.

And what of the outfielders, those other than wicket keepers? Here, by comparison, there are fewer opportunities to create records, but created they were. Walter Hammond, superb all-round cricketer, and slip fielder par excellance, had to be involved somewhere. His failure to make the '3,000 run club', and his lack of mention elsewhere, might lead one to suppose that he experienced something of a lean season with the bat — and you could say that by the standards of this extraordinary year, he did! In fact, the man who was to be England's leading cricketer over the next two decades, was just on the verge of greatness. 2,969 runs would, at most times, warrant special acclaim; in 1928 it put Hammond no higher than eighth in the averages. There was no one ahead of him on the winter tour of Australia, however, when the Test series there brought him a little matter of 905 runs, average 113.12.

But is is not so much Hammond the batsman that interests us here. Full commentary on both the player and the man, when at the height of his majestic powers, we shall reserve for another summer. A cricketer of abundant talent, he did not depend on sublime batsmanship alone to make his immense presence felt. Eighty-three Test wickets pronounced him somewhat more than a run-of-the-mill bowler; this perfectly-balanced, natural athlete missed little at slip. Certainly Hammond missed little enough this summer, and the 78 catches that went to hand still remains a record for a season. His ten in the match against Surrey has also never been approached. The loser here was A. H. Bakewell, whose eight catches, for Northampton v. Essex, would otherwise have equalled the record.

Ten catches in a match would in itself be satisfaction enough for most people; for Hammond, it was merely the centre-piece of a yet more remarkable performance — though not one you will find in the record books as such. In one glorious week at Cheltenham, Hammond the all-rounder came splendidly into his own; after such a week, who could have denied his right to the mantle of England's newest champion? Here, he revealed those sublime qualities that set him apart from lesser beings; here, one had an insight into the true measure of his greatness.

On the Saturday, Gloucestershire played host to Surrey. Hammond began by scoring 139 and, when Surrey batted, took four slip catches. In the second innings he made 143, held six more catches, and took the wicket of Jack Hobbs with a full toss! On Wednesday, the next visitors, Worcestershire, took first innings on a grey, humid morning ideally suited to swing bowling. Hammond, it seems, thought it so. Before lunch he took 9 wickets for 23, and caught the one batsman not to fall to his bowling. In the afternoon, he made 80 of Gloucestershire's 370–6, and then in Worcester's second innings, bowled unchanged to take six more wickets and two catches, seeing Gloucestershire home with a day to spare. 362 runs, 16 wickets, and 13 catches — not a bad return for a five-day week. Short of taking the gloves for a spell, it is difficult to see what more he could have done. If it was not quite Hammond's season, this was surely his week.

So you see, the summer was not solely an endless run-orgy, where bowlers toiled hopelessly in vain. Not only did the best, such as Freeman, reap a goodly harvest, but the game all-rounder also knew match-winning days. If Hammond was out on his own at times,* there were others not far behind, while from a birth-place some way west of Gloucester, a new comet was blazing across the cricketing sky.

You will recall our observation that this season was not noted for its Test series, and of the series taken as a whole that would be quite true. This was only the West Indies' second visit, and the first time they had

---

*I say 'at times' because as an all-rounder, Hammond did not correspond exactly to the general conception of that type. That is to say, he was very much a batsman first and then someone to whom bowling came easily, as did all things to this natural athlete. Had his batsmanship counted for less, Hammond would no doubt have devoted more time to his bowling. In fact, partly because he bowled at a brisk pace, but more so because England had greater need of his batting, he figured less in the dual capacity as the years went by. Nevertheless, on his day — and they were often — Hammond had few peers in this department.

been accorded three Tests. Though keen and uninhibited cricketers, they were scarcely a match for the better counties, let alone an England side that within a few months was to trounce Australia 4–1. Nevertheless, as we have come to expect, they did not want for individuals of great natural ability, individuals temperamentally suspect maybe, and thus a shade inconsistent — but ones who on their day could set a game alight. One such player of the 1928 party, gave every indication that he would continue to set matches alight for many tours to come — L. N., later Lord Sir Learie Constantine.

Constantine's place among the great all-rounders is not at all easy to assess. The young reader may search the records in vain to find his name amongst the likes of, say, Rhodes, Miller and Sobers and conclude accordingly that he was way down the list in more senses than one. But statistics, as we know, do not always provide a true, still less a fair, testimony of a player's skills, influence, or manner of playing the game. Brilliance cannot ultimately be measured numerically. Nor can a man's drawing-power; feats of rare athleticism are for the spectator — not the armchair pundit. Thus, more than most, Constantine's figures fail, to do justice to his cricketing magnetism.

In some senses, he was born at the wrong time. Not only were the West Indies new to the Test scene, but there was little opposition for them. South Africa was ruled out for non-cricketing reasons, which left only England and Australia against whom they could pit their talents. As a result, although Constantine took part in three tours to this country, a pitiful total of only eighteen Tests shows the extent of this legendary figure's opportunities at the top level.

Even so, breaking records for their own sake was never in his nature, though in the year-round nature of today's cricket, he would have accumulated them incidentally anyway. Constantine played cricket essentially for fun, flat out, as if each game were his last. His philosophy was simple: every ball had to be struck as hard, or bowled as fast, as possible; one should seek to be actively involved at all times. He was a showman, a born entertainer — and those who saw him would have found nothing wrong with that. Of magnificent eye, and with the lithe, rhythmic movements of the black athlete, Constantine's panther-like leaps in the field resulted in catches that few others could have made. Likewise, when advancing down the pitch, he uncoiled like a giant spring to meet the ball with the full force of his bat — a bat, one might add, that was seldom straight. If he made runs, they had to come quickly — only Jessop was faster overall — and, throughout 1928, his best year, he scored at a rate of 90 an hour.

Yet Learie was no out-and-out slogger, but rather a master of improvisation, seeming to have two strokes for very ball, the bat here, there, anywhere. The term 'you could not set a field to him', was no idle cliché in his case. One moment he would square-cut for six, the next, hoist the ball over the 'keepers head, while the straight clout over the sight-screen, the bat horizontal, made for refreshing variation. No one, I think, has ever hit the ball harder.

Again, when bowling, he put everything he had into deliveries calculated to beat batsmen for sheer pace, a cart-wheeling stump the aim every time. For these reasons, Constantine was never going to attain a consistency that makes for record aggregates. By the same token, comparison with the orthodox giants is an inappropriate one. Those privileged to *see* him, are in no doubt as to his standing among cricket's great all-rounders.

Not that any of this was known to us, when early in 1928 he was unleashed upon an unsuspecting public — not to mention those who had to face him. Constantine came with none of the reputation he brought to later tours, and one wonders if it was merely chance that he chose this phenomenal summer to produce such displays of all-round cricket. Whatever the explanation, the fact is that he did, and amen to the powers who ordained that it should be so.

In terms of cold statistics, of course, many of his peak performances would sound so similar as to risk undue repetition. This is perhaps to be expected of a man who knew only one way of playing the game. Two, however, stand out from the rest, and no worthwhile account of the 1928 season is complete without them.

In the match against Northamptonshire, Constantine gave notice of his powers by demolishing the home side's first innings in a dynamic spell of 7–45, including the hat-trick. Then, after scoring a whirlwind century, with five 6s, at well over a run a minute, he completed Northant's misery with a second burst of 6–67. That more or less, was that. It could be said, of course, that this was a weak county whom many sides put to the sword, but that hardly detracted from the brilliant manner of execution. Still, if a sterner test was needed to confirm his ability, then a Middlesex team that could boast of Hendren, Greville Stevens, Jack Hearne and other England players, was capable of providing it. They would certainly start favourites against Calypso cricketers unversed in the arts of the three-day game; indeed, word has it that Middlesex themselves saw the outcome as little more than a formality. They reckoned without Constantine.

Not that the man-of-the-match elect, was much in evidence during the county's first innings; nor at this stage, did the game promise to take anything other than a predictable course. Middlesex made over 350 runs much as they pleased, with Constantine mostly conspicuous for a dropped catch in the gully — while fielding at first slip! Still, that was the type of undistinguished start we had been brought up to expect from *Boy's Own Paper* heroes, and was not Constantine the epitome of one?

In keeping with the traditions of such tales, the side's fortunes were to sink very low, West Indies slumping to 79–5, before Constantine made his entry. He made 86 in an hour, and, after he was out, the innings somehow struggled on to 230. This was still hardly a healthy position and became even less so when Middlesex reached 98–3, to extend their lead to over 200. Now, Learie went on at the pavilion end, and, with some of the fastest bowling good judges claim ever to have seen, took 6 for 11 as Middlesex were shot out for 136. The target, then, was 259. Once again, West Indies' early batting failed, but a slight revival had taken them to 121–5 when Constantine once again took guard.

It all happened rather quickly. In a frenzied display of hitting, he reached 103 in an hour, taking West Indies virtually single-handed to their improbable three-wickets victory. His exhibition of sustained extravagant striking, can seldom have been equalled. Jessop comes instantly to mind as a rival, but even he did not hit the ball with quite the ferocious intent that Constantine demonstrated with every stroke. Some were truly astonishing, in terms of both power and manner of execution. One outrageous cut cum drive saw a good-length ball from 'Gubby' Allen dispatched clean over extra-cover and high into the Mound Stand. Another blow, hit with a flat and far from straight bat, hit the top of the pavilion rails with such force that the ball rebounded far into the enclosure, chipping paintwork and scattering the members. But however he hit them, or wherever they landed, Constantine enjoyed every moment of it. He was not alone in that.

While no one player wins a game on his own, Constantine came about as near to doing so as possible. Such days came but rarely, of course, yet he nevertheless contrived to enliven quite a few grounds that summer, hitting 37 sixes in his 1,381 runs, not a bad haul for a touring player. But, as we have stressed, it is not for huge scores Constantine is warmly remembered. Others have made more runs, played bigger innings; as many again have taken more wickets. But for sheer natural brilliance — the embodiment of 'sunshine' cricket, "There was," in the words of Hazlitt, "not only no one his equal, there was nobody second to him".

＊　＊　＊　＊　＊　＊

Naturally, there were many other fine contributions to this summer of plenty, perhaps all worthy of mention in less lavish times. But how do you follow Hammond and Constantine? Better to exit on a high note, though not without giving due attention to the regular honours board. Jardine, as we said, topped the batting averages, and handsomely. Yet, as further proof that even in a predominantly batsmen's summer, great bowlers were not without hope, a quickish lad called Harold Larwood headed the bowling list with 138 wickets at 14 apiece. Such economy would not come amiss at any time, but especially in this season when the going rate was 30 runs per wicket. But again, ten players achieved the 'double' of 1,000 runs and 100 wickets.

The County Championship went to Lancashire, who thus completed a hat-trick of wins — much to the disquiet of those east of the Pennines. However, only the most begrudging Tyke could claim that a side which had won fifteen matches and lost none did not deserve their success. Far sadder for Yorkshiremen, and indeed for all cricket lovers, was the death early that year of Roy Kilner, aged only 37, struck down in his prime by enteric fever. A great favourite as well as a fine all-round cricketer, Kilner had figured prominently in the great Yorkshire team of the early 'twenties, and it was not lightly said that Roses matches would never be quite the same again. Cricket, like life, has its triumphs, but also its tragedies.

That, so far as facts and figures go, fairly well tidies things up. To add that, some 250,000 runs found their way into the score book during that summer will hardly come as a revealing statistic, if like me, you haven't the faintest notion of the number made in an average year. On the other hand, the fact that no fewer than 414 centuries were made, will.

A season for all men? Some bowlers might not have thought so, but what of the paying customer? To compare one favourite year with another is, of course, a futile exercise. As always, it comes to a question of swings and roundabouts, taking your choice. For obvious reasons, 1928 could not match the feeling and atmosphere of, say, 1947, but against that, this richest of eras undoubtedly offered more great players. 1947 belonged primarily to two men, 1928 to many; two stars against a veritable Milky Way. Thus, each year must be judged on its merits and weighed accordingly. But there is nothing to stop seasons of very different character from being equally memorable. Back to roast beef *and* strawberries and cream again.

In the same way, presentation is bound to vary with each year. Here, for example, little attention has been given to mood, technique or detailed accounts. 1928 was not about mood and technique and such things; it was all about magnitude, records on the grand scale, everything being bigger and better than we had known — a season of rich pickings to which there seemed no end. And it is that aspect on which I have tried to convey.

Yet have we been quite fair? Carried away with a wealth of memorable events, it is all too easy to imagine 1928 as clinical and soul-less, devoid of warmth or finer feelings. It was not, of course. Cricket and sentiment go hand in hand; it cannot be otherwise, and by odd coincidence, in its own special way, this year showed us one reason why. How? By giving a welcome reminder of one of cricket's endearing qualities — that it is not essentially a young man's game.

Q. Surely many fast bowlers, although losing some of their pace, also become cleverer, canny, more thoughtful? For example: Trueman, Lillee, Holding, R. J. Hadlee. Is not that maturity too?

Indeed, fast bowlers (in some senses) apart, many players, like good wine, improve with maturity. The leading figures here illustrate that perfectly. Jack Hobbs, still the Master, was rising 46. Of those who made 3,000 runs, Woolley and Mead were 41, Hendren and Tyldesley 39, with Sutcliffe the baby at a mere 34. Freeman, the record wicket-taker, was 40 before May was out, while the man of that month, Hallows, answered to 33. None of them was under thirty, and some had careers that spanned the years from Grace to Bradman.

Yet here they were, still in command, and adding to cricket's charm. In this way, our idols, gods, or whatever they are to us, may be with us for twenty years or more — a goodly chunk of a man's life — and, in consequence, pervade a sense of permanence. Much more than with the stars of other sports, such as soccer, cricket's big names become a part of civilised life — no less so than morning papers or Sunday lunch. Their success or failure may influence our mood; their retirement brings a sense of loss, a sense that our world will be that much the poorer (England without Jack Hobbs was like beef without salt); their last match is a nostalgic, sometimes almost unbearable, occasion, where the eyes mist, and strong men affect to blow dry noses. We shared their careers; they were as friends, even though we may never have met them (the nearest I ever came to meeting Wally Hammond was when he trod on my foot at the Oval, but that is another story). Ultimately, we feel that with their going, a part of our own life has shut down too.

But, since age brings its benefits too, both in terms of matured skills and sentimental attachment, what better inscription to 1928 then, than that a season remarkable in every way should count so many old warriors among its heroes.

IV – A Gentler Age

Weather-wise, there were other fine summers in the years around 1928, but for one reason or another, none of them quite meets our purpose. 1930, for instance, was the year of Bradman — and Bradman — and Bradman. Now I have nothing personal against that gentleman. Indeed, with the benevolence that comes with dotage, I am prepared to concede that in Sir Donald, I witnessed one of the five best batsmen of all time — never mind who were the others. Equally, I can now acknowledge that a series which saw Australia abscond with our hard-won Ashes, contained much good cricket. But these are the charitable views of a mellowed mind. Unashamed patriot that I am, I could not honestly say that I saw much to enthuse over in a man who flogged England's best for double and triple centuries; nor about an Australian team that reckoned anything much under 700 to be a moderate score. Some people, it seems, just love to spoil other's enjoyment. That soul-less individual certainly did nothing for my peace of mind. No, unless you were a confirmed masochist — or an Australian, of course — 1930 would not come high on your list of favourite summers.

1933 was also a batsman's year, but now we were well into that 'too easy' era, mentioned earlier. Almost inevitably, it seemed, Hammond, Sutcliffe and Hendren all topped the 3,000-run mark, yet that apart, the season rather lacked for both incident and variety.

1934, on the other hand, because of overtones that had little to do with cricket, was spoiled even before it began. I refer to the Larwood fiasco. I do not propose here to re-tread well-trodden ground, but speak only of the effect upon this particular season. The fact was that, once again, we suffered the spectacle of England meekly surrendering newly-won Ashes, deprived this time of both Larwood and Voce. Thus freed from their persecutors, Bradman and Ponsford could again rattle up the big scores of old, yet one felt that even the Australians ultimately acknowledged that victory over such a toothless lion, was something of a hollow achievement. To make matters worse, Hammond, although averaging 76 around the counties, failed to produce any sort of form in the Tests. To say that this happens even to the greatest batsmen, which is true, was no consolation. What was consolation, however, took place at Lord's — Verity's match! On a rain-affected pitch, the

Yorkshire left-armer had figures of 15–104, including the wicket of Bradman twice — a welcome if short-lived triumph. All in all though, it was a somewhat unsatisfactory year.

If victory over the old foe were the sole criterion, though, one need go back no further than 1926, when, after seven lean post-war years, hopes were at long-last rewarded. Here, unfortunately, the combination of wretched weather and the shadow of a General strike served to make the success of that summer less satisfying than it might have been.

This is perhaps a good moment to qualify one of our leading principles. While it is true that no one relishes watching cricket under leaden skies, umbrella at the ready, inclement weather does not of itself rule a season out of the reckoning, as we shall discover. As we have stressed all along, ideals rarely take material form. In fact, the truly golden summers are few and far between, and, with all the other considerations, the cream years fewer still. It really comes down to this. If a wet season is memorable, then however else the weather may have affected us, it clearly did not spoil enjoyment, and may, dare one say, even have conspired to enliven the cricket.

It can happen, for instance, that timely rainfall produces a finish where non seemed likely; or provide a pitch that demands masterly batsmanship, such as we saw here from Hobbs and Sutcliffe in that historic Oval match. A tense dual between bat and ball can offer ample compensation for a delayed start. But more often than not, of course, as happened here, matches are badly curtailed or washed-out altogether, and too much of that sort of thing is frustrating for everyone. So, despite a gripping fifth Test that saw the Ashes restored to the Motherland, fine batting by the 'Old Firm' and three centuries from the quicksilver Macartney, four drawn Tests in a generally damp summer did not make 1926 a year over which to enthuse.

We must therefore look further afield, and our way takes us back among the treasure-trove of what is by common consent, cricket's Golden Age — 1896–1914. Now, as you might suppose, I have no first-hand knowledge of these times, and indeed the number who have must dwindle by the year. But is that really important? Cricket, after all, is historical matter, as much a part of our heritage as the triumphs of Trafalgar or Waterloo. And are these events any the less inspiring, simply because we were not there? The game's historians have not been idle, and from their graphic writings one can soon convince oneself that one is reading an eye witness account. Imagination is a wonderful thing — in the right place; and the right place is surely a cosy chair by the fireside in winter's depths, where for the cost of the clutched volume, you can be swiftly transported to a lighter, brighter world; perhaps, as here, to a glorious Edwardian era, the centre-piece of that enchanting Golden Age.

The Golden Age: How apt that title is when so many players bore that tincture, they formed a shining array, too detailed to describe in one breath, but containing such names as Ranji, Jessop and Trumper, not forgetting, of course, the Grand Old Man himself. That this was predominately the age of the amateur was so because their prowess demanded it. Certainly so far as batting was concerned. Heaven knows, there was competition enough from the professional ranks — J. T. Tyldesley, Hayward, Abel and later Hobbs and Woolley, to name but a few. Yet at the turn of the century, only Tyldesley among batsmen, could claim an England place as of right.

'Amateur' here, involved being something rather different from the latter-day conception of genial, hard-hitting county captains, who perhaps would not ordinarily make the side. W. G. and Co. were 'professional' in all but status, complete batsmen with a fluent, classical style founded yet on sound first principles — much like May, Cowdrey and Dexter of modern times. Amateur dominance was reflected in the batting averages. In 1905, for example, the middle of this period, they filled fourteen of the top twenty places, and this was a fairly typical year. Also, in Ranji and Jessop, this era produced two batsmen who could almost certainly be called unique.

The batting then, fashioned as much of it was at Oxbridge, simply typified the tenor of an opulent, if class-divided age, its main strengths necessarily lying with the privileged, but none-the-less gifted, amateur. Not so the bowling, however. Whether or not it was significant — it could be said that only payment would motivate someone to take on the rigors of six-day-a-week bowling — I could not say and rather doubt, but the fact remains that of the 'gentlemen', only Walter Brearley posed any serious threat to the professional's monopoly in that quarter. And what names he had to compete with; a galaxy no less glittering than the shining batting ensemble! Sidney Barnes, possibly the best bowler of all time; Wilfred Rhodes, whose record haul of 4,187 wickets has long stood the test of time; his great fellow-Yorkshireman George Hirst; Tom Richardson, Lockwood, Blythe — we could increase the list ad infinitum. The point surely has been made. The Golden Age was no mere legend no fond epoch created by the passing of time. As with any art form, there is always a classical period, and if one seeks the zenith of English cricket, it will be found here. One glance at the cricketing *dramatis personae,* in describing which we have as yet barely scratched the surface, should convince us that it was so. If not, then you are indeed hard, sharper, to please.

Not least, perhaps, this was a graceful age; not just cricket-wise, but as to the general trend of public behaviour. Whatever one's politics, there can be little doubt that most of us would welcome a return to Victorian values, if not to those conditions. Crowd trouble was virtually unknown. People went, strangely enough, for the purpose of watching cricket, and did so with none of the tiresome clatter that surrounds the game today. Spoiling other's enjoyment was not then a national pastime. Likewise, there was considerably better rapport, and unforced rapport at that, between players — particularly in Test matches — with far less gamesmanship and an almost entire absence of 'ungentlemanly conduct'. This is not to say that games were played in a frivolous atmosphere; players, as ever, gave all for their side; captains strove no less hard to win — but not at all costs. Yes, we know the great Bearded One was not above a little rule-bending, yet even he considered such artifices fair game — much as a schoolboy regards scrumping. Well, wasn't that just what he was — an oversized, lovable schoolboy?

And how amicable were relations between amateurs and pros? I am again on sensitive ground, but to those to whom class distinction and terms such as 'knew their place' have an offensive ring, all one can say is, it worked. Each in their way had respect for the other. As we have shown, the amateurs could bat a bit, and were not there by divine right, while the pro's deep knowledge of the game was oft sought by their skippers. Much like the services, the 'gentlemen' led, the 'players' faithfully did their bidding.

Again, it is unlikely that the traditional fixture between the two would have survived as long, or have proved as popular, had it bred any marked ill-feeling. Nor, until evolution reduced the amateur strength, were these games in any way one-sided. Evidence which suggests perhaps, that the division existed in name only — that all the Gentlemen were players, and all the Players, gentlemen.

As befitted a classic period, wickets in the nineties were perfected to accommodate the batting lords of the time. They were marble show-grounds; were not the flawless strips at Hove and Eastbourne expressly designed to exhibit the strokes of Fry and Ranji? Pitches were not lifeless, but firm and true. In the absence of rain, bowlers toiled hard for their wickets. This was the drawing-room cricket of a genteel, tranquil England, when news of Grace batting at Lord's filled the City's streets with Hansom cabs, and at Trent Bridge, to adopt a later phrase, it was 'Always three in the afternoon and 360 for 2'.

Cardus, I believe, used the phrase in *Days in the Sun,* printed earlier than the '30s.

And which of these fair seasons takes our fancy? 1895 perhaps — not strictly the Golden Age, but nevertheless a year in which W. G., at 47 years young, became the first player to achieve the coveted 1,000 runs in May. A year too, when Lancashire's A. C. McLaren took 424 off the Somerset bowlers, to record the highest score by an Englishman. Or 1905, when F. S. Jackson won the toss in all five Tests, and whose own contribution did much to bring about the defeat of Joe Darling's Australians?

No, for reasons of space we shall confine ourselves to just one season and not one of the fine ones either. Earlier, I hinted at a paradox — the exception to the rule that confounds all our ideals. This was 1902. It was said that one had no need of a water diviner that year, but should simply await the appearance of any member of the visiting Australian side. Then, as if on tap, rain would descend with unfailing regularity. Hardly a recommendation for inclusion in a work of this nature, I agree, but we did allow that if the cricket still shone through, theory might have to go by the board. Clutching at that slender straw then, and with brazen disregard of the number one qualification, I shall without more ado, plunge — an apt word — into what was probably the wettest season of the Edwardian era. For despite the fact that rain robbed England of almost certain victory at Edgbaston, any series in which one match is won and lost by three runs, another by one wicket, and which produces a century before lunch, is surely worthy of recall. Whatever else that summer lacked, there was certainly no shortage of excitement, nor indeed, wonderful all-round cricket.

V – Old Gold and Opulence

So far as Test series in this country are concerned, there has been none more dramatic than that of 1902. Moreover, if in Coronation year, King Edward's accession was not blessed with the best of weather, he at least had the good sense to ensure that it coincided with an Australian visit. After all, even a favoured prince cannot have everything. Not that he could have foretold the drama in store, though any cricket-lover could have told him that a side containing Trumper, Clem Hill, Monty Noble and — oh so many more Titans — was not here for the weather anyway. They were a powerful combination, as, indeed, they had to be in order to match the impressive talents ranged against them.

In truth, England would seem almost to have had an embarrassment of riches, and it remains one of cricket's great ironies that a year of abundant talent should see us forfeit the Ashes. But it was strongly felt, and with good reason, that had they kept the side that outplayed Australia for most of the rain-ruined first Test, England would have won by a margin, but loss of form by key players, injuries and a series of selectorial blunders, allowed the rubber to slip away.

Comparisons between players or teams of different eras, usually provide pleasant bar-room conjecture, but little more. It was a tribute then to England's strength at this time, that, by universal consent, the side named for the opening match is considered to be the best integrated eleven ever to take the field. Not the best possible — for one thing Barnes was missing — but the best to actually go into a Test. In order of batting, it read: McLaren (Capt.), Fry, Tyldesley, Ranji, Jackson, Braund, Jessop, Hirst, Lilley, Lockwood and Rhodes.

It is, of course, all very well to set down a list of names that, to we old-timers, still conjures a conclave of the Knights of the Round Table, but we are now four-score years on, and with time's passing, such players — much like Grace before them — are apt to slip into legend, to an age beyond our ken. I can well hear some saying to themselves: "Yes I know these names from the past, but they mean very little to me. How did they really compare with latter-day giants?" They might well ask. Answering them provides a glorious excuse to indulge in pen-pictures of the men who composed the golden eleven.

1. **Archie McLaren,** Lancashire. Captain and autocrat who led

England on 22 occasions, McLaren was an elegant opening batsman in the true classic tradition, a quality which prompted Sir Neville Cardus to assign him 'the noblest Roman of them all'. He scored five centuries against Australia, which not too many have achieved, but figures alone scarcely do him credit. Authorative, always looking to score, yet unhurried, McLaren assumed a commanding presence at the wicket, and his batting at no time made for dull viewing. Being the only Englishman to have played an innings of over 400 — and this in a three day match — says sufficient for his dominance at the crease.

As England's leader, his record is perhaps rather less distinguished, though it might be said that luck was not often with him. Remote, intolerant of lesser beings, and inclined to brusqueness, McLaren was not always at one with those under him. Remarks such as, "Oh God! Don't tell me you're playing," were not calculated to instil confidence in a trialist. But as a player, his place at number one was never in dispute.

2. **C. B. Fry,** Sussex and Hampshire. Surely a man for all seasons — an 'all-rounder' who could do a dozen things better than most people could manage one (how annoying he must have been). One of the finest scholars ever to leave Oxford, Charles Fry represented the university at both cricket and soccer, and only missed a rowing blue through injury; he also set a long-jump record that was to last for twenty-five years. He went on to become a double international, opened the batting and bowling for England, and be it noted, played for Southampton in the F. A. Cup Final of this year, 1902. One could also add a sizeable list of achievements in more serious fields, which would include poems published in *The Times,* and a naval career in which he rose to the rank of Commander, but it is worth as a cricketer that most concerns us here.

A proven athelete, Fry presented a fine figure of manhood, something betokened in his Olympian stance at the crease. Like all amateurs of the day, his game was founded on classical principles, though his economic style, with its absence of frills, perhaps made him less exciting than some of his contemporaries. Not that this worried Fry. When critics accused him of limited stroke-play, his tongue-in-cheek defence was: "Yes, I have only one stroke, but with it, despatch the ball to 22 parts of the field." Which in essence was true. He did not cut, as Tyldesley cut, nor leg-glance in the fashion of Ranji, but appeared always to present the full face of the bat, bringing it down through the same straight arc, and guiding the ball wherever he chose. A great theorist and thinker, Fry sought to achieve the optimum range with the minimum risk, and thus favoured the drive, at which he excelled.

With one stroke or not, a man who did not consider cricket his life, nor even his true vocation, he used it to pretty good effect. Even as a part-timer, it brought him 94 centuries, two hundreds in a match on five occasions, and, in 1901, 3,147 runs at an average of almost 80. Only Bradman and M. J. Procter share his distinction of scoring six consecutive first-class centuries, and Fry is one of but four men who have made a thousand runs in each of two months in the same season. That stroke certainly found every corner of the ground.

Though he never toured abroad, Fry later led England to victories in this country, when his shrewd brain made him an able captain. This would be quite enough for most of us, but not for him. He went on to write several books on the game, including his autobiography *Life Worth Living*, took his place at the League of Nations Conference, and at one time was offered the kingship of Albania.* Yet Fry took most satisfaction from his work on the training ship Mercury, where, with his wife, he spent his latter years preparing boys for the navy. A visiting friend once said to him: "This is a fine show C. B., but for you, a backwater."

To which the Commander replied, "It depends on whether one wants to be successful — or happy."

Fry never lost his zest for life and retained much of his remarkable agility to the end. In his youth it was said, he could, from a standing position, spring on to a Victorian mantelpiece; at seventy-three, he could still run upstairs five at a time. In fact, having few inhibitions, he was always liable to borrow a stranger's umbrella to demonstrate how to play this or that stroke. His was a marvellous character, and if this portrayal has strayed beyond its main purpose, it is simply because Charles Fry was a truly exceptional man. They just don't make them like that any more. A 'Life Worth Living' it surely was.

3. **J. T. Tyldesley**, Lancashire. The only professional to command a place in the top five, Johnny Tyldesley numbered among the very best batsmen on turning wickets, and was possibly the finest cutter the game has ever seen. He was, of course, well-equipped all-round, the complete player in every way, but that particular stroke — like the 'Compton sweep' or the 'Cowdrey paddle' — was Tyldesley's speciality. There have been many fine cutters of 'cuttable' deliveries and, equally, many who played the stroke well on true wickets, but he would cut the

---

*He is said to have refused the offer on the grounds that he would rather be an English gentleman than an Albanian king.

good-length ball and if it pitched on middle stump, on an unpredictable pitch, it made no difference. A risk, then, to play him at number three? Tyldesley calculated that the runs it brought him, set against the times it got him out, well justified the risk involved. And 86 first-class centuries makes for powerful argument.

McLaren, Spooner, Tyldesley. Has any county, one wonders, ever boasted a better first three in the order? Lancashire and followers were indeed fortunate to possess a trio of such high quality, a trio who complimented each other so well. When one had admired the constrasting merits of McLaren's imposing splendour and the delicate grace of R. H. Spooner, what better prospect than a swordsman's innings from the nimble-footed, business-like Tyldesley. And if both openers failed, who more likely to retrieve the situation? Some of his finest innings were played in difficult conditions, when all about him had fallen victim to the pitch, and he was left to play almost a lone hand. On any number of occasions his contribution, whether large or small, constituted a vast proportion of the side's total, and he was, without a doubt, the best bad-wicket batsman in England at this time.

No finer illustration of this could be found than in his innings at Melbourne in 1903–4, where on the worst of 'stickies', it was said that only one batsman on each side played as if they'd ever held a bat in their hand. Tyldesley made 63 out of 103, Victor Trumper, 74 out of 122 — both with a quickness of foot that made batting seem a different art, both unflinching as the ball reared about them. No less a judge than Sir Pelham Warner regarded these as the best innings he had ever seen on a bad wicket.

Loyal patriot though he was, proud to honour his country, Tyldesley's love for his native Lancashire went deeper yet. A local favourite, his was the most familiar figure in the side for many a day. Nineteen times he made over a thousand runs in a season, exceeding 2,000 in four of these, and 3,000 in one. A safe and vigilant fielder in the deep, Tyldesley remained on his toes throughout the longest innings. Anything less than highest endeavour in a job for which he was paid and loved, was to him unacceptable. He was at all times a credit to his calling.

There are few stories about him — he was not that kind of man — but one seems to have a moral. Although he scored thirteen double centuries, Tyldesley never played an innings of 300. Once, when on 296, he remarked on the fact to the opposing skipper, who in the spirit of things, asked his bowler to 'toss one up to him'. The good man duly obliged, and with by far the worst ball of the day, bowled Tyldesley neck-and-crop. One likes to think that at heart he did not quite relish the idea of being made a present of the target. Be that as it may, both as a player and a man, Johnny Tyldesley had the respect of everyone — a true gentleman among professionals.

4. **K. S. Ranjitsinji**, Sussex. His name, colouring and rank alone, would have sufficed to make Ranji a special attraction. The day was then far off when an Asian neighbour was commonplace. One doubts if the average Edwardian ever encountered an Indian, let alone on a cricket field, and still less one who was a prince. Full of Eastern promise — much to Sussex's delight (and one might say Fry's) — Ranji brought a mystique that both warmed and enchanted a curious public. Slender, lithe-limbed, with dark, piercing eyes, his influence was such that no one would have been surprised had he performed the rope-trick at the wicket.

Ranji did not quite oblige them with that feat, but nevertheless conjured a few batting 'tricks' of his own to hold crowds equally spellbound. We ventured that he was unique, and few, one feels, would argue with that. No one, but no one, played the leg-glance so fine, so late or with such consummate ease as did Ranji — nor yet with a timing so exquisite that the ball sped like lightning to the boundary. Some would tell you that the turf was left scorched in the wake of its path, but that, perhaps, is carrying legend too far!

What we might take as fact, however, is that those burning eyes were among the keenest. Reliable witnesses claim that Ranji could discern the stitches on the ball in flight — something not perhaps out of the question when one considers the way he literally flicked it out of the 'keeper's gloves, or followed round so late as to deflect the ball between 'keeper and slips. And this against the fastest bowling, the bat's blade turned with the barest movement of supple Asian wrists.

Again, though, we speak of but one specialist stroke. So much is made of Ranji's leg-glance that one is apt to think of him purely as a rich entertainer, which he certainly was, rather than the supremely well-grounded batsman that history tells us he had to be. You did not aspire to England's number four berth on charm alone. Like Tyldesley, Ranji took runs all round the wicket. One thinks of the latest of late cuts, again played well after the ball was past him and drives of a velvet delicacy that yet raced deceptively to the farthest boundary. And every stroke from a bat that might well have been a wand — such was the magic of the man. All the more sad then, that 1902 was not his year. Never at ease on the consistently damp wickets, Ranji was unrecognisable as the player one knew him to be. This was that depressing season that comes to most men at some time or other.

But in any case, Ranji's quality cannot be reckoned by sheer weight of runs — as with most of this side. Great players should not be judged solely by career aggregates, which may depend upon many factors. More pertinent, is how, when and against whom those runs were made. A connoisseur's fifty has more value than many pedestrian hundreds. Had Ranji never made a century, he would have endeared himself to the public no less. In fact, though, he scored seventy-two of them. In a relatively short career, 3,000 runs in a season twice, suggests something more than fleeting brilliance.

Ranji seldom toured abroad and, incredibly, played in only 15 Tests, his best innings almost certainly being his dazzling 154 at Manchester in 1896. No one else on the England side achieved much that day, but Ranji batted in festival fashion. He was, however, most at home in Sussex, where his liaison with Fry offered bowlers a daunting prospect. He not only ran up double-centuries, but, without a hint of boastfulness, promised them in advance, usually to atone for an earlier failure. Many are the stories surrounding this legendary figure, but one I am quite prepared to believe relates to his Cambridge days.

Ranji, who would go anywhere for a game, once turned out in a local match played on commonland. After making a hundred, he wandered off to watch another game, and, finding them a man short, promptly stepped in and obliged with a second century before returning to field for his own side. Going in again, he proceeded to make this third three-figure innings of the day. One doubts if that little feat has been performed too often.

Yet, as said, it was not for quantity of runs that Ranji is best remembered, but for his power to entrance with the pure magic of exotic batsmanship. A prince in every sense of the word.

5. **F. S. Jackson**, Yorkshire. A very fine all-round cricketer and tactician, whom many believed should have been awarded the captaincy ahead of McLaren. Indeed, some went so far as to say that had Jackson been at the helm, England would not have lost the rubber, a belief strengthened by the fact that three years later, he led the side to a comfortable victory over what was virtually the same Australian XI. This is pure hypothesis, of course, yet, with hindsight we know that Jackson was the most consistent performer in both series, his form in the second of them unaffected by the burden of captaincy.

Colonel the Hon. Sir Francis Stanley Jackson, P.C., G.C.I.E., as he later became, was another perfect example of the cricketer whose career figures are woefully misleading, one whose true place among the greats can only be gauged subjectively. Jackson was essentially a part-timer; he did not captain his county and never toured abroad. Test matches were relatively infrequent and, like Ranji, his number of caps, 20, provides no guide to his ability. Thus, although 'Wisden' can tell us that he still managed five Test hundreds, and older editions no doubt do credit to his deeds, the name of F. S. Jackson nowadays tends only to appear, and that often, in the section headed, 'Cricket Records'. Well, as Mark Twain said: "There are three kinds of lies — lies, damned lies, and statistics."

One must delve deeper to discover Jackson's standing among Test cricketers. A product of Cambridge, well schooled in basic technique, he was building on the foundations of a natural games player, whose straightforward approach to cricket made batting appear the easiest thing in the world. Jackson neither feared bowlers nor disrespected them, but treated each ball on its merits. He played all the strokes, but always chose the obvious one; he knew only one way to play and did not adapt to meet different conditions or the state of the game. For him there was never a crisis, only the next ball.

This is why, no doubt, he was so often the man for such a crisis; a player who can make runs when they were most needed, is invaluable and Jackson was such a player. At number five, he was needed either to retrieve a poor start or to play an innings that would put England into a winning position. In his inimitable way, he was rarely found wanting. His performances in this series will be described later, but in 1905 he topped both the Test batting and bowling averages, scoring 492 runs, at an average of 70.28, and taking 13 wickets at 15.46. Jackson is in fact, one of the few players to have a higher batting average in Tests, alone nearly 49, than in all first-class cricket combined, Sutcliffe and Leyland being the others. A man for the big occasions, clearly.

As a bowler, he is perhaps underrated. Jackson's figures bear no relation to his ability to take good wickets, and when most needed. Right-arm, on the brisk side of medium, he was good enough to share the new ball, and was the bowler most likely to break a partnership. It was a poor match indeed, if he did not do something with either bat or ball.

Because of other commitments, he led England in just the one series, but, after calling correctly in all five Tests, remains probably the only captain never to have lost the toss! He was certainly a successful one, a natural leader who took the job in his stride. Cricket was not primarily his life, any more than it was Fry's, and, like his great contemporary, he was destined for more worldly fame. A promising parliamentary career was temporarily suspended when, in 1914, as Commander-in-Chief of the West Yorks. Battalion, Colonel Jackson went in to face a rather more hostile attack. He survived to become Financial Secretary to the War Office, and later, Governor of Bengal — posts which he occupied with distinction. Beyond argument, Sir Stanley Jackson served England well, both as a fine cricketer and a distinguished citizen.

6. **L. C. Braund,** Somerset. Perhaps one of the less charismatic names in this side, Len Braund was nevertheless the steady, consistent all-rounder England required in the middle order. However, with bat or ball, he was more than merely competent, and could have commanded a place in any county side on the strength of either batting or bowling. He was also the finest slip-fielder in England. There being many different types of catch, it is never easy to say which was the best, but one of Braund's must rank among the most astonishing. A ball of some speed was turned by the batsman, Clem Hill, in the direction of fine leg. Braund at first slip, flung himself across to take the catch one-handed while suspended horizontally in mid-air. Poor Hill had to be told by the wicket-keeper what had happened before dragging himself off in dazed disbelief.

A measure of Braund's ability as a batsman can be gauged by the fact that he came in ahead of both Jessop and Hirst, even when the former functioned purely in that role. Possibly not so exciting as some of those around him, he could still be a bold stroke-maker when the need arose. He also bowled the leg-break with a high degree of skill, which gave variety to an attack that was well-equipped for all contingencies. Douglas Jardine always maintained that a player should not be judged on his best figures, but by how he performed on the most demanding occasions, which, in those days meant playing against Yorkshire. By that criterion, Braund passed the test handsomely.

In the three years, 1900–02, Yorkshire lost only two matches, both times remarkably, to lowly Somerset. In the first of these, Braund shone primarily as a batsman, he and Lionel Palairet laying the foundations of a total that saw Somerset to a comfortable victory. It was in the second match a year later that Braund showed himself to be a match-winning all-rounder. Of the forty batsmen dismissed, only four achieved double figures — Braund twice, his scores of 31 and 34 being the highest in each innings. The beauty of being an all-rounder, of course, is that conditions must suit you in one area or the other. Thus, having batted against the odds, Braund now let his hair down to run through the Yorkshire innings with 6–30, followed by an even better spell of 9 for 41! He bowled unchanged throughout, by which time Yorkshire had grown rather tired of him.

Nor had he quite finished. In the return game, where Yorkshire scrambled home by one wicket, Braund bowled 79 overs in taking ten wickets, with the champions glad to escape from Taunton undefeated. For England too, he often came good when it most mattered; not always spectacular, he was a handy man in any capacity. His mere presence in the slips gave bowlers heart, and one should not forget that it was his bold innings of 102 that paved the way for R. E. Foster's historic 287 at Sydney in 1903–4.

What you will not find in the record books, however, is that Braund was the best of travelling companions, the ideal tourist who did much to relieve the tedium of cross-country treks; a good-hearted man, always ready to console a dispirited colleague. Sadly, he was to suffer an illness in later life that necessitated the amputation of both legs. Yet he still went regularly to watch the play, and remained cheerful to the end. Len Braund, the happy cricketer.

7. **Gilbert Jessop,** Gloucestershire. One of cricket's uniques. Of players who have made over 20,000 runs, Jessop was unquestionably the fastest scorer of all time. But as that aggregate indicates, it would be wrong to call him a slogger. A long-handle merchant might, in one priceless innings, thrash his way to a hundred and beyond; but not 53 times as Jessop did. On four occasions, he even did it twice in the same match. E. B. Alletson's celebrated knock — 189 out of 227 in 90 minutes — has for long taken pride of place among fast-scoring records, yet he never came near to repeating that feat again. Jessop not only bettered it with 191 in the same time,* but also hit five double-centuries, and only once batted for more than three hours. In fact, only ten times in his whole career did he bat longer than two.

Make no mistake, Jessop was a genuine batsman — a rare, highly unorthodox one, maybe — but a batsman just the same. He played all the orthodox strokes, plus a few of his own, and against all types of bowling. The better the length, the better he liked it; the faster they bowled, the harder he smote. He was neither the hardest nor the longest hitter of the ball; he simply hit it more often than anyone else. The reason is not hard to find. Jessop was not restricted by tight or defensive bowling. With a combination of eye and lightning footwork, he made each ball hittable, and while that might be said of any batsman

---

*Alletson's innings is placed first probably because it was the more sensational in the latter stages. He scored the last 139 runs in under forty minutes, the last 89 coming in a quarter-of-an-hour.

who uses his feet, it still calls for pretty special reflexes to effect a pull, cut, or straight drive for six while several yards down the wicket. Few, if anyone, could hope to follow his example.

From a crouched stance, head lowered almost to the bat handle — hence his name the 'Croucher' — Jessop took a sighting of the flight, then catapulted forward in a rapid chase towards the pitch of the ball, and with a long sweeping down-stroke, flung the bat at it, arms at full length, but with wrists back-locked, and unloosed at the moment of impact. This takes somewhat longer to describe than Jessop required to carry it out. In this way, he could despatch the ball over the ropes anywhere in the arc between square-leg and backward point. If they then dug it in short, he just lay back and cut and carved off his stumps or eyebrows with equal disdain. "Couldn't bowl to him," was no idle observation.

Not only could they not bowl to him, but no captain could safely gauge a declaration with Jessop in the opposition. He made nonsense of all reasonable calculations, as many a sporting skipper found to his cost. An hour of 'The Croucher' and the issue was usually beyond doubt. Few were prepared to take the gamble; he came off too regularly to make it a favourable risk. And this was the signal difference between Jessop and the slogger — the frequency with which he produced his sustained onslaughts. He, in fact, holds few of the *acknowledged* fast-scoring records. C. I. J. (Big Jim) Smith has made the quickest *genuine* fifty, Percy Fender the swiftest *genuine* hundred,* while others have perhaps gone along faster at some stage of an innings. But in terms of consistent big hitting — which allows little margin of error — no one has ever come close to emulating Jessop. Hence his right to be termed unique.

If his most famous innings was that played at the Oval in this Test series, then others, no less entertaining, lacked only the drama of the big occasion. His 101 in forty minutes for Gloucester against Yorkshire in 1897 was technically the fastest, but that 191 in only one-and-a-half hours, ten years later, was the more numerically astounding. Although the Gentlemen of the South against the Players of the South, at Hastings, was in the nature of a festival match, that is not to say that the bowlers were not trying! No professional relishes being hit hard and often to the ropes. Nevertheless, they watched helplessly as Jessop rattled up 50 in twenty-four minutes, 100 in forty-two, and 150 in just over the hour. He so dominated the strike, that his runs came out of 234

---

*Smith's achievement has been beaten and Fender's equalled but only under inauthentic, not to say, dubious circumstances.

scored while he was at the wicket, the whole side being dismissed for 313. In those days, the ball had to be struck clean out of the ground to count six and this Jessop managed five times, while many of his thirty fours went full-pitch into the crowd. This latter is another point one is apt to overlook when assessing bit hitters of the past. His figures would have been even more impressive under the 1910 amended ruling.

Ready examples of Jessop's smiting powers are legion, but this should be sufficient to indicate the threat he posed to bowlers. Jessop himself, a modest man by all accounts, did not attribute his capacity for long-hitting to any special gift, but did add that he never suffered from nerves, nor was he influenced by the state of the game. He went for his strokes almost from the start, and gave no heed to circumspection, either before or after a break. This is borne out by the fact that his fastest hundred occupied twenty minutes either side of the luncheon interval! No doubt had he sought to play himself in, and picked the correct balls to hit, Jessop would have made more runs and returned a higher average than his overall 32, or his Test average of only 21, but would the game have been enriched as a result? As it was, he assured himself a notable place in cricket history — and, need one say, a rightful place at number seven in this most auspicious of sides.

8. **George Hirst,** Yorkshire. A great-hearted and tireless all-rounder, Hirst was the best-loved of all Yorkshire cricketers. Others have been championed for their prowess on the field, but no one, by dint of both triumphs and the manner of their attainment, endeared themselves to northern folk as did George Herbert Hirst. He simply enjoyed playing cricket, but more, was seen to enjoy it, and he maintained that if you batted as well as bowled, then you enjoyed yourself twice as much. And there's a good deal of truth in that.

What he did not say, was that one also had to go through twice the amount of work, but then if one was as good as he was, one performed twice as many outstanding feats. Truly, Hirst's achievements with bat and ball were stupendous, his figures surpassed only by his companion and life-long friend Rhodes, and even he never managed to score 2,000 runs and take 200 wickets in a season, as did Hirst in 1906. Whether this record will ever be repeated is doubtful but whoever does so, "will" in the holder's own words, "be bloody tired!" By way of a trial run, incidentally, Hirst had topped 2,000 runs and 100 wickets in each of the previous two seasons. In all, he scored a 1,000 runs in a season nineteen times, took over 100 wickets fifteen times, and accomplished the 'double' on fourteen occasions. In all he scored 36,203 runs and took 2,739 wickets.

All of which might lead one to imagine — as I once did — a picture of a strapping, leonine figure, after the fashion of most dual-purpose cricketers. Not so. Hirst was of no more than medium height — square-shouldered, certainly — but in no way resembled the brute stature of, say, an Armstrong, Miller or Botham. Rhodes was not a big man, of course, but then he did not bowl at pace. Hirst did, and all day if need be — borne along by an outsize heart and a deep love of Yorkshire. He, probably more than anyone, epitomised the earthy, play-to-win flavour of Yorkshire cricket, prepared at all times to sell his life dearly. His reserves of stamina were seemingly inexhaustible, and there is not room here to list even half the occasions when he bowled unchanged through an innings, or with cudgel-like blows, steered his side out of trouble.

His success as a bowler owed much to the prodigious swerve he imparted, and when at one stage of 1902, this ability allegedly deserted him, Hirst was dropped for the fourth Test. England lost, and indignant Yorkshireman declared it to be poetic justice. They had a point. It was not so much whom you replaced him with, as with how many! Quite apart from his skill with bat and ball, Hirst was the best of all mid-offs at a time when that area needed much defending. No player is indispensable, but great all-rounders come closest to entering that category; and George Hirst was a great all-rounder.

If his figures for England do not quite match his county record, that is only relatively so. For Yorkshire, Hirst was a colossus; for England, merely invaluable. True, at Test level he did not make his hundreds, nor run through sides as was his wont, but there was no one England would rather have had at the crease in a crisis, while on the plumbest wicket, his late-swerving deliveries often reaped success where others toiled in vain. At all events, the selectors saw the error of their ways and restored him for the fifth Test, a decision, as we shall see, that was fully vindicated.

More than just a great cricketer, Hirst was a legend in his own time, and his 1904 benefit haul of £3,703 remained a record for over twenty years. For all his fighting qualities, he was a mild-mannered man, with an air of rough gentleness about him. Though he gave his all and played the game hard, he had no wish to win at all costs. To Hirst, it was still a game, and to be won by honest effort within the bounds of fair play. If he appealed, it had to be with justification; intimidatory tactics were not for him. Nor, by word or gesture, did he signal his displeasure. A list of the great all-rounders would, it is fair to say, find his colleague Rhodes at the top. But if George Hirst were not second-best, and only narrowly at that, then I don't know who was.

9. **A. A. Lilley,** Warwickshire. Even at the worst of times, England have never wanted for world-class wicket-keepers, and it would indeed have been strange if a time of plenty had seen a deficiency in that department. In fact it did not. In 'Dick' Lilley, England had a stumper who ranked with the best — a man as assured of his place in the Test side, as was Godfrey Evans fifty years later. Lilley was not so exuberant as Evans, nor as busy as Knott, say, but unobtrusive, and quietly efficient, much in the manner of that doyen of Australian 'keepers, Wally Grout. In his youth he had stood up to the fast bowlers, as was the custom of the day. Men like Blackham and Gregor MacGregor would have considered it cowardly to do otherwise, but on the advice of no less a personage than W. G. himself, Lilley then took to standing back — on the not unreasonable grounds, that stumping chances were negligible, he would take more catches, and that it was altogether a less risky proposition.

To show that we do not believe that everything in days past had superior merit, this sensible method eventually became the standard practice that we associate with the modern game. Old habits die hard, however, and for a good while there were many who remained scornful of Lilley's new-found safety-first approach. Why did he need pads and gloves to take the ball in the region of long-stop, they scoffed. Effectively his answer was given by his holding on to the England job for twelve years, in which time he made 35 appearances — a fair number in those days.

Lilley went about his work without fuss, taking catches with a calm assurance, and stumping his victims with a quiet politeness that deemed it almost a pleasure to be put out by him. In Test cricket he dismissed 84 batsmen, which is a slightly higher ratio than Evans achieved with his 219 in 91 Tests. His value to the side did not end there; Lilley was a sound competent batsman who went in high in the order for his county, and continued purely in that capacity when his wicket-keeping days were over. He was also a fine reader of tactical situations and well steeped in cricket lore — had he not, after all, 'kept' to all the best bowlers of the time? Arthur Augustus Lilley was not out of place in this company.

10. **William Henry Lockwood,** Surrey. One of the famous Surrey fast bowling trio of the nineties — Richardson and Lohmann being the others — Lockwood was now entering the twilight of his career. Thirty-four years of age, and born when Grace was a slim-line athlete, he almost belonged to a different era. Almost, but not quite. Very much an in-and-out bowler, he could either do nothing wrong or little right;

1902, in fact, saw him at something approaching his very best. In style, he was the complete antithesis of Richardson, yet as with so many fast-bowling combinations, the contrast made the partnership more, not less, effective. Where Richardson equated to Keith Miller or Fred Trueman — a fiery whirlwind who hurled himself at batsmen — Lockwood more resembled Lindwall or Statham, gliding in with a smooth, controlled run-up, yet being equally capable of perpetrating spells of destruction.

Again like Lindwall, he was a more than useful batsman — a brave hitter who got his fifties against the best. Yet such was his temperament, that, seven years earlier, Lockwood had seemed a finished cricketer. In 1895 he took only 60 wickets against Richardson's 290, and did virtually nothing with the bat. However, the next six seasons saw a revival of fortunes, and in 1902 he was indisputably England's number one fast bowler.

All the more mystifying then, was that he should be dropped for the Sheffield Test, in which England were soundly beaten. Yet another bizarre decision was acknowledged on all sides as a major blunder. Hastily reinstated, Lockwood thereupon proceeded to make his point, yet it seems inconceivable that this should have proved necessary. Every Test series has its share of controversy, and we can all be wise after the event, but the dropping of Lockwood has to go down as an error of the first magnitude. On his day he could be devastating, a positive match-winner. And 1902 was without doubt, Lockwood's 'day'.

11. **Wilfred Rhodes,** Yorkshire. One of the very greatest of cricketers, and surely the best number eleven of all time! Of course, had Rhodes' potential as a batsman been recognised early enough, he would never have occupied that lowly berth, but even so, in this side it is hard to see that he would have rated higher than eight or nine. Yet here was a man, who in England's service was to fill every position in the order, the pinnacle of his career coming ten years later, when he found himself opening the innings with the mighty Jack Hobbs. Their stand of 323 at Melbourne, on the 1911–12 tour, still remains a record for the first wicket in Anglo-Australian Tests. In all, Rhodes scored nearly 40,000 runs — only twelve have bigger aggregates — and while his 2,325 in Test cricket may not seem over-large by today's standards, to average 30 at this level, playing against only the best, places him high on the list among pre-war players. And this was, and still is, cricket's leading wicket taker — a man who would have walked into the England side even had he never made a run.

To describe Rhodes as a very great cricketer is clearly not to exaggerate. In fact, those words seem hardly adequate when one speaks of a player who in a career spanning more than thirty years, acquitted himself in three different roles. After first coming to light as a top-class slow left-arm bowler who could 'bat a bit', the next years saw him develop into a genuine all-rounder, who twice scored 2,000 runs and took 100 wickets in a season. Then, although losing four peak years to the First War and aged well over forty, Rhodes re-emerged to re-stake his claim as a front-line bowler, his late recall to the England side in 1926 (he was then 48) doing much to clinch a match that brought home the Ashes.

Like Hirst, Rhodes was the embodiment of Yorkshire cricket, and for much of the Golden Age these two in harness formed the backbone of a county side that took the championship seven times. But prolific as was Hirst's yield in Yorkshire's cause, Rhodes for the most part, did even better. In each of 23 seasons he took over 100 wickets, 21 times passed 1,000 runs, and 16 times performed the 'double' of 1,000 runs and 100 wickets. One fancies also, that a career aggregate of over 4,000 wickets will take a lot of beating.

What really gave Rhodes the edge over his colleague, though — that fine margin which separates the very, very good from the top-most strata — lay was his ability to reproduce that form in the more demanding climate of Test cricket. Here one can add 127 wickets to the runs already mentioned, his figures of 15–124 at Melbourne in 1903–4, being among the more notable feats in Test history. But as valuable, perhaps, as his proven ability with bat and ball, was the shrewd cricket brain that accounted for much of his success in removing good batsmen. Also, towards the latter stages, when his physical powers were on the wane, his profound insight maintained him as a testing opponent. Such was the respect accorded the 'high priest', that long before his playing days were over, he served as a Test selector, and it was, in fact, at Rhodes' own suggestion that he played in that vital fifth Test in 1926. Which not only tells us that, at nearly fifty, he had no obvious peer, but also reveals something of the man himself.

Of true Yorkshire blood, Rhodes personified the pithy, blunt, no nonsense character of that ilk. A stern adversary, he was equally uncompromising with those about him, and little given to false modesty. More than once he was heard to remark after a match, "that they should have put him on sooner". No doubt he was right — few had his appreciation of how best to use conditions or wickets. A law unto himself, but only because his stature earned him that privilege. He was perhaps not unique in the sense that Ranji and Jessop were unique — that is to say, highly unorthodox. Quite the reverse in fact. As a bowler, Rhodes had the perfect, easy action of the classic slow left-armer; his batting, if unpretentious, conformed to textbook principles, his technique sound. But, in terms of all-round achievement and contribution to the game, one doubts if we shall ever see his equal. The absolute master of his craft, Rhodes probably more than anyone served to exemplify the 'professional' cricketer. Number eleven in this side was no rabbit.

Who would disagree that this was England's best-ever turn out? Entertainment was certain with batting right down the order, all eleven having made a century in first-class cricket, and 500 between them, with eight also having a Test hundred to their name. A five-man attack did not want for variety, providing genuine pace, fast-medium cutters, swerve, leg-breaks and slow left-arm spin; Lilley behind the stumps had no rival at this time, and all were natural fieldsmen.

What of those other contenders left out? Barnes, as we say, was unavailable, and although at this time fairly new to Test cricket, would, as possibly the world's finest bowler, no doubt have been an original choice. Who would make way for him is another matter. In a career of only twenty-seven Tests, Barnes took 189 wickets and it would be surprising if anyone has ever had a higher striking-rate. It means, roughly, that had he played the same number of games as a present-day bowler such as Willis, his tally would have topped 550. Though inclined to be temperamental, a fit Barnes would hardly have weakened the side.

Only he might have claimed a place as of right, but look at the men who were either passed over or who made just the odd appearance. Among the latter, the 'understudies', were the Surrey stalwarts, Tom Hayward and Bobby Abel, and the stylish L. C. H. Palairet of Somerset. Hayward was among the foremost of professionals, with twenty caps already to his credit, and could perhaps be considered unlucky not to have gained a regular place at this time. Although a little on the slow side, with his best years yet to come, Hayward was a heavy scorer and, moreover, consistent in county cricket. Ninth in the all-time aggregates with 43,518 runs, including 104 hundreds, he exceeded 1,000 runs in a season twenty times, going on to make 2,000 runs eight times and 3,000 twice. The 3,518 runs he scored in 1906 remained unsurpassed until the coming of Edrich and Compton. Hayward is also one of the elite who have made 1,000 runs before the end of May,* a feat

*Not *in* May, since 120 of his runs were scored in April.

he accomplished in 1900. Yet in 1902, this solidly consistent opening-batsman made just one Test appearance.

Likewise his county colleague Abel, though at 45 years of age, with his Test days well behind him, his selection was something of a gamble anyway, and must be seen as one of the less inspired choices. 'They never come back' is an old boxing axiom that might equally apply to cricketers. A man may reasonably continue in Test cricket until well into his forties, but to return after a gap of six years at that time of life, is an adjustment few can make. Doubtless, the selectors were influenced by Abel's overall record. He had made over 30,000 runs, including 74 centuries, his 357 against Somerset in 1899 being the highest innings by a Surrey player. Having figured also in two first-wicket stands of over 300, his ability as an opener was scarcely in question.

Nevertheless, that was county cricket and, more to the point, in the past. To ask him now to step into the cauldron of a Test arena was, one feels, expecting too much of a game but aging war-horse. And so it proved. Here it seemed, not for the first time, the selectors had lost their way; there were times in this series when they appeared to have lost their reason.

The selection of the third batting replacement, Palairet, who played in the last two Tests, certainly gave less cause for criticism, though it is puzzling that he was preferred to Hayward in view of the latter's vastly greater experience. Still, Palairet's selection was quite logical, if not wholly successful, with no harm resulting to the player himself. An amateur, not dependent on cricket for his livelihood, Palairet was not in any case destined to spend long in the game. For all that, he was a fine player, delightful to watch, and not even Spooner surpassed him for sheer grace. If he did not quite come off in the Tests, there were others with bigger reputations whom this wet summer did not see at their best either.

There were others too, with bigger reputations, who were not even considered: R. E. Foster, who eighteen months later was to make the highest Test score by an Englishman in Australia; J. T. Hearne, whose 3,061 wickets has been bettered by only three players; Pelham Warner — Foster's captain on that tour — Albert Trott, C. J. Burnup (he did get to be twelfth man) Arthur Shrewsbury, but why go on? We have proof enough that the eleven who performed so well in the one match for which they were all chosen can justifiably be considered the best-ever, and that necessarily a good many fine and even great players were therefore forced out of contention. And had that side stayed together, or more relevantly, played to its potential, the inquests which arose as a result of England's unlikely defeat, would have been unnecessary. These inquests, sad to say, thrust poor Fred Tate, that unhappy victim of circumstance, under the spotlight's glare. His one Test appearance ensured him a permanent place in cricket history, though not, alas, one he would have chosen.

But we are racing ahead. In the high optimism of June, no one, least of all the selectors themselves, had cause to envisage the sorry chapter of events that were to cloud that series, especially after the spectacular happenings of the first Test.

VI – Rubber Remarkable

So, as the rubber of 1902 got under way in a spirit of optimism, it seemed that the only clouds on the horizon were those in the sky. Rain, in short, was never far away — the all too familiar story of the summer. With wickets not subject to protection, batting would never be easy; an innings of 50 or 60 would often prove a priceless score.

We shall not dwell over-long on the early matches, for in the best show-business tradition, the high drama was saved until last. At Edgbaston England, batting first, had got off to a poor start, with McLaren, Fry and Ranji all out, and only 35 on the board. But Tyldesley, the man for a crisis, was still there, and, with Jackson, another who relished a fight, saw England past the 100 before Jackson's plucky innings came to an end. Tyldesley then took command, and, by the time he was eighth out for a splendid 138, had taken England to the respectability of 295. Lockwood (52) and Rhodes (38) added an unbroken 81, enabling McLaren to declare late on the second day with the score 376–9. Overnight rain had in fact delayed the start until three o'clock, and the atmosphere was still heavy with moisture when, some time after tea, Australia began their reply.

No doubt England had enjoyed the pitch at its best, yet no one was quite prepared for what happened next. In less than ninety minutes, Hirst (3–15) and Rhodes (7–17), tumbled out a palpably strong Australian side for just 36 runs. Though Rhodes did most of the damage, it was Hirst who first opened the door, his enormous swerve posing problems with which only Trumper, who made 17, seemed able to deal. This probably contributed, as it often does, to wickets falling at the other end. 36 all out remains Australia's lowest completed Test match score.

Following on, Australia had reached 8 without loss, when, frustratingly from an English point of view, rain prevented any further play in the match. (These were three-day games, of course.)

If fortunate to escape with a draw, Australia could at least take heart from the brief glimpse of mastery shown by their number one batsman. Many judge Victor Trumper to have been Australia's finest-ever player on all wickets, and although his score here was, in itself only a small one, he gave clear indication of his capacity for making deadly bowling look highly playable. In the months to come, he made a mockery of greasy wickets and dank conditions, his 2,570 runs being the most scored in that season by any batsman, English or Australian. But Trumper did not merely score runs; he made them with superb artistry. 'Wisden' had this to say about him: "No one has at once been so brilliant and so consistent since W. G. Grace was at his best; he seemed independent of varying conditions, being able to play just as dazzling a game after a night's rain as when the wickets were hard and true." What finer testament could a player receive? However, in the Tests, he was given little chance to shine before the Sheffield match.

England were never again to touch the heights of Edgbaston. Perhaps that was to expect too much anyway, but whatever the reason, the combined effects of injuries, loss of form, and the mysterious ways of the powers that be — all worked to destroy the balance of a well-integrated side. The second game at Lord's was virtually a wash-out. England again made a disastrous start, losing both Fry and Ranji for ducks, but McLaren and Jackson, scoring at a run a minute, took them to 102 before rain again forced an abandonment.

Bramall Lane at last produced a result, though to English eyes, a most disappointing one as Australia romped home by the comfortable margin of 143 runs. Whilst it is true that their victory was based largely on the superlative batting of Trumper and Duff, and some fine bowling by Noble, the incomprehensible decision to leave out Lockwood was poorly received by those who watched England struggle to take wickets. Even Rhodes, who finished off Australia's second innings with four wickets in 19 balls, was not brought on until late in the day, and the general feeling was that England had contributed much to her own defeat.

And so to Old Trafford — arguably the most recounted match of all time, though not, alas, entirely on account of the enthralling cricket that took place. Not that the dramatic events of a truly gripping encounter have themselves failed to make history. Sir Neville Cardus and his like have certainly done justice to them. What one means is, that the outcome hinged less upon England's performance on the field, than actions taken off it, and an issue that refused to die can hardly escape mention. (As if we did not, in any case, love a bit of altercation.) Here, a match which lacked for nothing in entertainment, is yet more renowned for a personal tragedy, for the sorry result of what transpired to be without doubt the most highlighted, the most chronicled and most ill-fated selection in cricket history — one destined to have far-reaching consequences, and one the hapless player himself lived long to regret.

The Fred Tate saga is, of course, well-known — how circumstances conspired to make him the scapegoat for England's defeat. Yet somehow — perhaps for the same reasons that sell newspapers — one finds the pros and cons of a major incident too intriguing to pass off in a word. It was all so dependent upon the cumulative effect of small quirks of fate — each unremarkable in itself, and, for the most part, causing little comment at the time. It was certainly unfortunate that Hirst should choose this moment to lose his swerve, but, while the dropping of a player well worth his place as an all-rounder brought widespread recrimination, his replacement was not, as yet, the object of undue criticism.

In fact, prior to Old Trafford, few outside Sussex gave much thought to a highly able but unsung county off-spinner; nor indeed as Tate went about his honest duties could he have remotely foreseen that the belated reward for years of loyal service would lead him to be cast in the role of villain. But on the helpful wickets of that year, Tate had been enjoying quite his best season, taking sweet revenge for the nought-for-plentys that were the normal lot of his kind. At thirty-five, he must surely have long relinquished all hope of England honours, yet at a time of great strength, from nowhere, came his big chance. Deputy for the mighty George Hirst.

There were, up to a point, sound reasons for Tate's inclusion. As a bowler pure and simple, he was the man in form, week-by-week reaping a goodly crop of wickets, while years resigned to toiling on plumb pitches had made him well-practised in the art of containment. A disciplined professional, he pitched a faithful length and waited patiently for the 'good' days. At such times, Tate would rub the ball in the dirt, and whittle his way through sides, but he was seldom unplayable. A solid county performer — no more, no less.

There was the case for the selectors, and had the need been for a supporting bowler, no more might have been heard. But the man Tate replaced was something more than a change bowler, something more than just a specialist bowler altogether. Hirst's absence left a deficiency in all departments. Viewed in that light, it is difficult to see how Tate presented the best alternative. A safe fielder at slip he may have been, but he was strictly a tail-end batsman. He might hold up an end for a while, but that was the best one could hope. This hardly made for favourable comparison with the country's leading all-rounder. But McLaren pressed strongly for Tate's inclusion, and as a co-selector, the captain's vote carried the day.

The early stages of the match did not involve him overmuch. He suffered no more than the rest when Australia took first innings, and Trumper, at his brilliant best, proceeded to conjure a century before lunch. Lockwood, Jackson, Rhodes and Braund were all treated as village-green trundlers as, almost apologetically, Trumper, in two hours of breathless stroke-play, cut the cream of English bowling to ribbons. As modest as he was talented, this prince of opening batsmen had none of the ruthlessness of Bradman. He did not 'hate' bowlers, but rather took pity on them. They were there merely to toss him his meat and drink — and on that first morning he displayed a rare appetite.

A batting wicket — easy runs perhaps? Not a bit of it. Though the pitch was not spiteful at this stage, traditional Manchester weather provided grey light, a damp atmosphere and a sluggish outfield. Added to which, runs from these bowlers had always to be earned. No, Trumper in this form simply made cricket look a different art, made run-scoring look the easiest thing in the world, all bowlers reduced to a common mediocrity. When he was out the transformation was abrupt. While Trumper was there, the runs flowed and a big Australian total seemed assured. Well supported by Clem Hill, he saw them to 173–1. At that score, however, he was dismissed for 104 and, once he had gone, an attack that had until then looked innocuous, went through the rest of the batting to such good effect that Australia were restricted to a total of 299. The reprieved Lockwood had taken 6 wickets for 48.

Australia's score, however, began to assume larger proportions when, not for the first time that summer, England's early batting crumbled, five wickets going down for just 44 runs. But, again not for the first time, Jackson led the recovery, and with Braund put on 141 for the next wicket, after which contributions from everybody saw England finish only 37 behind on first innings. Jackson's defiant 128 showed all his fighting qualities, and, if a contrast to Trumper's matchless showpiece, was scarcely less important. Thanks largely to him, England were back in the match.

Now though, the weather which had always threatened, brought about a complete change in the game. With one day remaining, a draw had seemed the most likely outcome, but heavy overnight rain on an already soft wicket put a very different complexion on things. This was not yet a turning pitch — it was too damp for that — but a greasy, two-paced surface on which the ball would cut through, skid and lift off a length from anything above medium pace. A drying wind gave promise of better conditions later on, but the first two hours could prove decisive.

The extent of Australia's reliance on Trumper was seen again, his cheap dismissal throwing the innings into disarray. Lockwood was even more devastating than in the first innings, running through the early batting to finish with figures of 5–28. In fact, until the arrival of Joe Darling, the Captain, a rout on the scale of Edgbaston looked probable. Seeing little to be gained from defending, Darling, as Australians have always tended to do, elected to hit his way out of trouble, and, with a few lusty blows, quickly ran into double figures. Then, with his score at 16, came the first significant incident in Fred Tate's tragedy.

With Lockwood for the moment rested, Braund was trying a few overs of spin. His fifth ball brought Darling, a left-hander, to the striker's end, and Palairet, who always stood at square leg to Braund in county games, set off on the long jaunt across the wicket. But McLaren impatiently gestured him back, saying that it was not worth switching for one ball, and beckoned Tate round to that position on the leg side. On such simple decisions are matches sometimes won and lost.

Darling, looking to make hay with the slow bowler, and knowing he was hitting with the spin, treated the last ball to a good old-fashioned hoick to leg, putting all his weight into a shot intended to clear the ropes. But he got under it, getting more height than distance; this was a straightforward catch, surely, for the lone sentry posted for the stroke. Indeed, had Tate stayed his ground, he would have had the simplest of catches, but the flight deceived him, the ball — as it always will with the spin imparted by the left-hander's pull-stroke — curving away behind square-leg before straightening.

Thus, Tate, thinking the catch would elude him, made ground to his left, only to see the ball check, and then descend quickly to the spot he had just vacated. In that fleeting moment all was lost. Though recovering sufficiently to get both hands to the ball, his impetus at full stretch caused him to spill it on to the turf. Poor Tate. He was a good fielder close to the wicket, but this was not his position. The swirling skier calls for good judgment born of long practice. Though McLaren muttered his disapproval, was he not guilty of paying insufficient attention to detail?

However, the miss did not appear to have been costly. Although Darling went on to make a robust 37, the whole side was out for just 86. England's second innings task looked no more than a formality: 124 to win in a possible four hours, though, with rain constantly threatening to take the players off the field, that equation could always be upset. If England were to square the series, runs would have to be made while they could. Still, the pitch was probably easier than at any time during the day — only relatively though — and the heavy roller would help to deaden it for a spell. Barring a deluge, victory seemed reasonably assured.

Clearly those sentiments were shared by McLaren as he sought from the start to have the match quickly won. First with Palairet, then Abel, the captain set out to force the pace while conditions favoured. Then, perhaps with an anxious eye on ever-darkening skies, he aimed an over-ambitious stroke and holed out at cover. 63–2. Half way there, and a wealth of batting to come.

Ranji was next to the middle, but, oh, how he struggled. Never can he have edged, or played-and-missed, so often as he did here. In a stay of half an hour, a player whom people flocked to watch poked about uncertainly for just two runs. 92–3 — and suddenly, runs appeared very hard to come by. Abel had been in for some time, yet looked anything but comfortable, and even Tyldesley found difficulty in getting the ball away. No signs of panic yet though. Thirty-odd runs to find with 7 wickets in hand; defeat inconceivable.

Nevertheless, when two more wickets fell in quick succession, the odds against the impossible happening had shortened considerably. This time moreover, there was to be no rescue act from the middle order, Jackson, for once, failing, and Braund dismissed just when he seemed to have settled in. Even so, at 109–7, four good hits were all that was required. Lockwood could apply the long-handle, while both Lilley and Rhodes were well capable of seeing off the runs. Oh for Jessop, who might have got them in one over, but he, of course, was not playing. Nor — nobody needed reminding — was Hirst. Not for the first time in the match, his presence was sorely missed. 'Someone had blundered.'

This was emphasized when Lockwood, on whom hopes of a quick finish rested, made not a run. Flurries of light rain were becoming more frequent, and the weather could yet have had the last word, but from a once commanding position, a draw for England would hardly be a satisfactory result. In any case, a win was necessary in order to keep the rubber alive.

To that end, Lilley, at least, made clear his policy, favouring the bold, assertive approach, rather than simply waiting for the runs to come. There was something to be said for this. Bowlers now well on top were not prone to the loose delivery; the stranglehold imposed as the innings faltered would not be broken by cautious methods. On a wicket which had already claimed eighteen victims that day, the defensive push offered no guarantee of survival anyway. Better to die fighting was patently Lilley's reasoning.

Intention is one thing, however, execution quite another, and, in the face of some splendidly tight bowling, supported by fine out-cricket, his efforts to force matters tended to be more frantic than fruitful. To their credit, Trumble, Saunders and the rest had stood firm in the face of a seemingly hopeless task. Looking no more than steady while McLaren was dictating play, their persistence had at length brought its reward. Lifted, as bowlers always are by the fall of quick wickets, they were now men transformed, every ball pitched on the spot and threatening to do something off the wicket, a wicket, moreover, never firm from first to last, and not improved by three days of wear and tear. At best, run-scoring was not easy; scoring them quickly — as Lilley's inability to assert himself now showed — asked a good deal more.

The tension mounted. Rhodes at the other end, as always, remained cool in a crisis, content merely to take the single whenever he could. No heroics were forthcoming from that direction; he was not that kind of cricketer. A man of iron nerve, he was not, or did not seem to be, affected by tension. He would see it quietly through to the end, come what may. In their different styles, the two contrived to wrest seven priceless runs from an attack grown miserly with success. 116–8 — just eight more wanted, but, now again, fate took a new turn.

Lilley had the strike. A ball, pitched perhaps a shade further up than intended, came on to his swinging bat with that sweet sound which tells of a stroke hit straight and true. It went up and up sailing towards the pavilion, a six-hit all the way. Or was it? Certainly, it would clear the ropes before pitching, but was not someone careering round the rails like a man possessed? Clem Hill! "What spirit! But he would never catch it," cried those nearby. Yet catch it he did, to a stunned silence, and at full tilt, his momentum carrying him a full twenty yards past the spot. For just a split-second, time seemed to stand still, and then the ground erupted to wild cheering, as friend and foe alike — at first unable to believe the evidence of their own eyes — realised that they had witnessed the catch of a life-time. Some said the ball actually crossed the line, and was blown back by the wind. That is just possible; we cannot say. It was, in any event, a stupendous piece of fielding, and poor Dick Lilley was out to the best shot he had played — perhaps ever played. 116–9, 8 still wanted, and who now, for all the bats in Lilleywhites, would have been in Tate's shoes?

Consider. Here in his first Test, it fell to him, a county number eleven, to save not only the match, but also the series. More experienced men might not have relished the prospect. Again, he had barely reached the middle, when a heavy shower drove the players indoors, where for what must have been an interminable forty-five minutes, he sat huddled in the dressing-room, mentally rehearsing his strokes and no doubt agonising over the missed catch that had made his nightmare journey necessary. No one surely, has had a worse baptism.

On the resumption, Tate would have to face an entire over, unless he could manage a single. If he could just stay there and leave it to Rhodes, the feeling was that England would still get home. 'Block, block and block again', everybody willed — the silent urgings of a crowd at fever pitch. The hopes of a nation rested, it seemed, on Tate's shoulders, as, amid unbearable tension, he pushed forward to safely negotiate the first ball. Audible relief. The next he failed to middle, but that hardly mattered as it edged away through the slips for four. Halfway there. More excitement; one more snick would do it. He could yet be a hero.

But to the last the gods had toyed with him. Two balls later, Tate was completely beaten, and turned to find his stumps shattered. England had lost by three runs. Tate would live to play that ball many times in the days to come.

An astonishing match was over. That England had managed to lose a game there for the taking took a good while to sink in. Questions had to be asked, of course, just as they were sixty years later, when, on the same ground, another batting collapse saw the Ashes thrown away.* Then, as now, Australia had not so much won as been presented with victory; then, as now, harsh criticism followed. This was not the routine post-mortem that follows any inept performance. Here, the feeling was that something very like treachery had been committed; in the aftermath of frustration and disappointment, an incensed public were making their anger felt. They sought a scapegoat and for heads to roll.

At a time of great strength, the flower of English cricket had twice been trampled in the dust — both times it was generally thought, without the best side available. But whereas at Sheffield, England had never looked like winning, and had had the worst of the luck, here at Manchester, the sense of certain victory snatched away, added to the galling margin of defeat, gave much more cause for wrath. It was too tempting to think hypothetically — if Hirst had played in place of Tate; had McLaren taken more care with his field placings; if Hill had not

*In 1961, when Ritchie Benaud retrieved a 'lost cause' against Peter May's side.

taken that incredible catch. It was, of course, easy enough to account for a deficit of just three runs. But at the end of the day, though the selectors were roundly admonished, and the captain did not go unscathed, the only long-term sufferer in the whole sad affair was Fred Tate.

It is history how, that night at Manchester station, he felt that people were pointing him out, and thereafter fell into deep dejection. How on the journey south, his friend Len Braund, tried to console him, and, in so doing, ventured to make the most erroneous sporting prediction of the century. "Don't take it to heart Fred," he urged; "It will all be forgotten in a week." But Fred Tate would not be consoled and, of course, Fred Tate was right. It was not forgotten in a week, nor a month, nor throughout his life-time. Nor could he put it out of his mind. Though he went back to bowl as well as ever in his county's remaining games, he left cricket at the end of his best season and took a licensed premises at Haywards Heath. A bowler, at his pace, might have wheeled away for another ten years. But in failing for once as a cricketer, he seems to have felt that he had failed as a person. Too ready to blame himself, remorse drove him from the game he loved, and which he had served so well.

And what had he done to deserve all this? Tate's 'crimes' eighty years on, do not exactly make sensational reading. Summed up, he bowled tidily if unspectacularly, and took two wickets; he missed a horrid, swirling skied catch when fielding in a position to which he was not accustomed; with the bat he did what any self-respecting number eleven might have done — took four off the edge, then got out. Not altogether the stuff of villains. Men have made worse debuts and not paid so dear a penalty. It all seems so irrational, until we remember that life, particularly where it concerns a man's deepest feelings, usually is.

But it is ironic that a series which produced so many good things and so many great moments, should be best remembered for a failure; that a match which saw a century before lunch, some heroic bowling, and a catch of rare athleticism, should be clouded in such a way. But 'The Test that Fred Tate lost' it will always be. They sought a scapegoat, and he was ready-made for the job. An extreme example, one fears, of a familiar story; the case of the good county man in peak form, pressed into Test service, and failing to bridge the gap between the two — with no one more harmed than the 'honoured' player himself.

But, from the deepest sorrow, joy. The good news here was that from the depths of one man's misery, a new star was born. At least, on this latter point, that is what we would like to believe, and have no reason to doubt the word of so reliable a witness as Leonard Braund. He said that on the gloomy train ride south, Tate had rambled on wildly about making amends for his failure, saying he had a seven-year-old boy at home who would one day put the matter straight for him. Braund, thinking his friend distressed and not quite himself, took little notice, but as we now know, Fred Tate was once again proved right. Twenty-two years later, son Maurice made *his* Test debut — with a rather different outcome. He took a wicket with his first ball, and 4–12 in the innings, he and Gilligan dismissing South Africa for 30. His first year in Test cricket brought him 65 wickets, and, for the next few seasons, Maurice Tate carried the England bowling almost single-handed. Father Fred was well and truly vindicated.

The rubber was won and lost; dead it was not. Every bit as exciting as the Manchester game — with none of the controversy — the cliff-hanger at The Oval perhaps ranks alongside the famous tied match between Australia and West Indies as the most thrilling of all. Here was another example of cricket's unique attraction, with each day and each match an event in itself. The urge to win can still be great, even if nothing hangs on the result. Here England badly needed to salvage something from the wreckage; Australia, as always, were keen to underline the margin of their superiority.

There should be no doubt that, leaving aside England's self-inflicted wounds, these were two fine and evenly-matched sides. Had both teams batted in similar conditions throughout, one thinks there would have been little between them. So morally, if not, with Australia holding a 2–0 lead, arithmetically there was still, so to speak, everything to play for. Even so, no one could have envisaged this see-sawing, heart-stopper of a match that surely belongs to the realms of schoolboy fiction. But back to the start.

England fielded probably the strongest side they could muster — that is, on the evidence of current form. Neither Fry nor Ranji were chosen, but so poor was their showing in this series — they averaged four apiece — that their omission brought few complaints. Palairet therefore kept his place as McLaren's opening partner, and Hayward came in at number four. After the lessons of Manchester, only an outsize mental aberration would have led the selectors to leave out Hirst, so with Jessop also back, the team showed only two changes from that of the golden eleven of the first Test. However, this seemed of little account when Australia won the toss, and, batting consistently right down the order, occupied the whole of the first day in reaching 324 — a score generally considered 'safe'.

Indeed it looked all of that and more, when heavy overnight rain consigned the side batting second to the worst of the conditions — a regular feature all through. England were up against it from the start; no one really settled in, and at 136–8 they looked certain to be asked to follow on — which, on this pitch, spelt inevitable defeat. With 38 still needed, Lockwood, who since his reinstatement had hardly put a foot wrong, joined Hirst — the other reject. As tense a struggle as one could envisage then ensued. It needed but one mistake by either man and England's hopes would probably be in vain. Slowly, with a single here and a two there, they edged to safety, though with little enough to spare. The follow-on averted, they added a further 9 — England all out 183, 141 behind on first innings.

But now it was Australia's turn to be put through the hoop. Again Lockwood was to the fore, taking 5–45 in a torrid spell in which he made the ball fly alarmingly off a length — a sight that must have made England's batsmen thankful they *had* saved the follow-on. As it was, they were still in with a chance, and Lockwood, who had taken eleven wickets at Old Trafford only to finish on the losing side, was doing his utmost to keep that chance alive. The major batting gone, it did not take long to mop up the tail, and, early on the third day, Australia were all out for 121. For England, an excellent fight back; yet Australia had the runs in the bank. Chasing 263 in the fourth innings still left them with much to do. Too much thought some, who felt that Australia's first innings score could prove decisive.

That opinion seemed to be only too-well founded when, in little more than an hour, England lost the wickets of McLaren, Palairet, Tyldesley, Hayward and Braund for a paltry 48 runs. The match looked as good as over; notwithstanding the later batsmen's proven ability, 216 from the last five wickets on this pitch, and after such a start, rated a very tall order indeed. But Jackson — what a saviour that man was — was now joined by the unpredictable Jessop, and these two, first looking to get a good sight of the ball, set out to restore the innings.

The thought of Jessop playing himself in places some strain on the imagination, but here, *by his standards*, he showed watchful restraint during the early overs, his first twenty runs taking nearly as many minutes. But now, as if suddenly deciding that the bowling held no terrors for him, he cut loose in a display of destructive hitting such as has rarely been seen on a Test ground. Jessop's first fifty came at a run a minute, his second in precisely half that time, as bowlers who only moments before had looked deadly, were hammered to all parts of the field. It had to end, of course, but by the time it did, after just seventy-five breath-taking minutes, Jessop had dramatically altered the state of the game. 187–6, last man 104.*

Jackson, normally no slouch himself, made only 35 out of a stand of 139, but with Jessop gone, now took control of the innings. Ably supported by Hirst, he steered England to the brink of victory, though they still had a little to do. Jackson's departure again opened the door for Australia, and when the ninth wicket went down, 15 runs were still needed. We all know how Hirst was supposed to have said to Rhodes: "Come on Wilfred, we'll get 'em in singles," and the fact that it is not strictly true, makes it no less stirring a picture. At any rate, get them they did, and who cared how? As Hirst said years later: "At such times you don't know what you do say." All that mattered to most was that, amid great excitement, England had staged a remarkable and historic recovery, coming back to win a match in which they had always been struggling, and where at one time all seemed lost. That it made not one scrap of difference to the rubber, had nothing at all to do with it.

It would be reasonable to assume that in the shadow of a fiercely competitive Test series, the county scene was comparatively tame. This was not entirely so. There was nothing to match Jessop's heroic charge at The Oval, or Trumper's bedazzlement of Old Trafford, but then these were rare gems for which one might wait an age to see. Nevertheless, there was much to enthuse over. For Yorkshiremen, this marked a rich period in their county's history — one of quite a few. The year 1902 brought them their third championship in succession, in which time, as stated earlier, they suffered only two defeats, both at the hands of Somerset, or, more specifically, Len Braund. No one else, however, gave them much trouble this season — not even the Australians. Two weeks after Hirst and Rhodes had skittled them for 36 at Edgbaston, the tourists encountered Yorkshire at Headingley. An even worse fate befell them. This time it was Hirst and Jackson who did the damage. In just fourteen overs, Hirst (5–9) and Jackson (5–12) shot out a full-strength Australian side for just 23 runs, thus virtually

---

*Jessop's first and only Test century remains the second-fastest ever at international level. J. M. Gregory's for Australia against South Africa at Johannesburg in 1921–22 came five minutes quicker.

ensuring a famous Yorkshire victory. Again, these figures make it hard to conceive that Hirst could be dropped by England.

There surely was definitive proof that it is bowlers who win matches. Hirst, Rhodes and Jackson, together with Scholfield Haigh (brisk off-breaks) represented as daunting a combination as any county has been privileged to have, not excluding Surrey's great match-winning quartet of the fifties. Then too, we recall, the champion county humbled Australian tourists, but without detracting from the wonderful performance of Laker and Lock in that match, Ian Craig's 1956 side was below-strength and soundly beaten in the Tests, whereas, as we have seen, that of 1902 proved more than a match for England. By that yardstick, Yorkshire's was slightly the better of two fine achievements.

Such was their supremacy that summer, that they totalled three times as many championship points as the runners-up, Sussex. But if York-shire were out on their own, every county had its big names, and none were dull. Even Hampshire, the wooden spoonists, had in C. B. Llewellyn an all-rounder who scored, 1,000 runs, took 170 wickets and was among the fourteen from which the side for the first Test was chosen. Certainly Sussex, with Fry and Ranji at the crease, were not tedious to watch. Nor were Lancashire, with McLaren, Spooner and Tyldesley, plus the bowling of Barnes and the colourful Walter Brearley to entertain. Nor, of course, were you likely to be bored by Gloucestershire when Jessop was on the rampage. Worcestershire had the Foster brothers, of whom R. E. was the most brilliant; Somerset, besides Braund and Palairet, boasted that legendary squire of the West, 'Sammy' Woods; Notts had their big Gunns — William and George — in addition to Arthur Shrewsbury; while Middlesex, for a side without an England representative, positively glittered with box-office attractions.

Cosmopolitan by tradition, the team from Headquarters has never been short of 'imported' players — nor indeed of unconventional ones. Thus, this era brought together such widely diverse talents as P. F. Warner, the epitome of the classic amateur; the somewhat more extrovert Albert Trott,* a big-hitting Australian all-rounder who succeeded in playing for both countries; J. T. Hearne, whose considerable tally of wickets we have already touched upon, and the less orthodox B. J. T. Bosanquet — father of the late Newscaster Reggie — who, in perfecting the 'googly', made a little news on his own account.

Trott, or 'Albertrott' as he became known, was alone well worth the admission money. He was a sort of Erik Satie of cricket. Always liable

*Tragically to die by his own hand.

to do something out of the ordinary, his short career was a catalogue of rare and sometimes unique feats, for which he seemed to have a liking. If one allows that he was a bona fide all-rounder — that is to say, worth his place as either batsman or a bowler — his exploits with the ball were all the more astonishing. For example, in 1900, all ten wickets in an innings against Somerset. Trott is by no means alone in achieving this bowling nicety, but you can be sure that the vast majority to have done so were specialist bowlers.

Even so, he was not content with plain, unvarnished accomplishment. His four wickets in as many balls against Somerset — again — in 1907 was nothing new, but how many, we wonder, have done it in their benefit match — and performed the hat-trick in the same innings! Clearly this flourish had been saved for the big occasion, for these were the only hat-tricks of his entire career. A fine sense of timing.*

Likewise, Trott's aggregate figures demonstrate scorn for the commonplace. Not a few players have scored 2,000 runs and taken 100 wickets in a season, worthy effort though it undoubtedly is, but only four have managed the reverse, that is, 200 wickets and 1,000 runs. Trott did it twice and was the first to do so. Again, curiously, as if he regarded this as the pinnacle of achievement, these are the sole instances of him performing the normal 'double' of 1,000 runs and 100 wickets. He was not to know that first Hirst and then Maurice Tate would both set new targets.†

As a batsman, Trott did not in fact, do himself justice — we have Jessop's word for that. Like that other illustrious figure, Trott was a consistent hitter but, in Jessop's opinion: "Had he only curbed his impetuosity, he would have graced any team, for he had moments when he looked far removed from a hard-hitting batsman of haphazard methods." Or in the less flattering terms of his county captain, McGregor: "If he'd only had a head instead of a turnip . . ."

"But, as with all long-hitters, including Jessop himself, prudence was not in Trott's make-up, and without doubt the spectator gained as a result. As it was, he spent most of his playing life attempting to clear the Lord's pavilion and, although never quite managing it cleanly, he several times came close to doing so. The first recorded effort was in May 1899, when he hit the very top of what was to him the left-hand tower. Had this massive blow been a few feet to the right, it would have

---

*If not of accounting, his exploits brought the match to an early finish, thus depriving himself of extra 'gate' money.
†Hirst's unique 2,000 runs and 200 wickets we already know about; Maurice Tate three times in seasons 1923–5, took 200 wickets and scored 1,000 runs.

fairly sailed over. However, this seems not to have satisfied him, and a few weeks later, he succeeded in striking the coping work of the roof* itself, from whence the ball disappeared from view — much to the perpetrator's immense relief. Though he hit high and often ever after, these twin blows were the nearest Trott came to attaining his ideal.

His best remembered feats of 1902 included a huge drive over extra-cover, which landed high up in the Mound stand (regarded as incredible by no less a judge than Sir Pelham Warner), and an innings of 103 out of 136 in seventy minutes — against, of course, Somerset — that included 17 fours. Many of these 'fours' would be worth six today, notably one hit to square-leg off Braund that soared clean out of the ground. No, the county scene was scarcely dull with men like Albert Trott around.

Surrey's great team of the nineties was now perhaps a little past its best, yet players like Hayward, Abel and Lockwood still made them a force to be reckoned with. In Hayward's benefit match against Yorkshire, no fewer than 1,427 runs were scored for the fall of just 24 wickets. Friendly bowling to suit the occasion? We know better than that, with Yorkshire's formidable foursome on parade, and with Lockwood, who took 7–159, enjoying his best season. Could it have been that all were simply out to entertain? Or was the entertainment simply a by-product of playing the game skilfully and properly?

Mention of entertainment calls Kent readily to mind. For long the advocates of bright, yet graceful, cricket, the Hop county were rapidly bringing together the side that reached its peak during the Edwardian years, though they had to wait for the coming of Woolley before acquiring the final seal of greatness. If they achieved nothing of note in this season, Kent still had their fair share of crowd pleasers. Colin Blythe had the most beautifully rhythmic action of any slow left-arm bowler, and was second only to Rhodes among contemporaries. Too delicate, it seemed, for the rigors of sport, his approach suggested more that of a Paganini at work. Long fingers curled lovingly round the ball, Blythe bowled with all the passion and sensitivity of a musician indulging his art. So too with his temperament. He hadn't Rhodes's fiercely competitive instincts, nor quite his consistency, but such can be the way of genius. On his day he could be unplayable, and he was to have quite a few 'days' — one could say literally. In a single day in 1907, he took 17 Northants wickets for 48 runs, including 10 in an innings, and there can be fewer better days than that. Even his 15 for 99 against South Africa in the same year, took him a few hours longer.

*As a result, this enormous blow, like the earlier one, counted only four, not six.

Yet his havoc was wrought without 'malice'; like Trumper, that other aesthete, Blythe did not 'hate' opponents. No, in him one saw purely the artist keyed to concert pitch, lost in his performance. Strictly 'not for competition, but for exhibition only'. Sadly, as with many men of inspiration, Blythe had a short life, just thirty-eight years. Nonetheless, for fifteen of them, he truly graced the fair fields of Kent.

Kent's batting was not yet as strong as it was to become but it was attractive. J. R. Mason, C. J. Burnup and S. S. Day were fine amateur players, and in the case of the last two, not only in cricket either. For did not these sporting polymaths form the left wing of the mighty Corinthians, who in this very year took on, and beat, the F.A. Cup winners Bury, themselves 6–0 winners over Derby County. This was indeed a romantic age.

No doubt Sussex followers thought it so. Not only did their county finish second in the championship but, in a wet summer, contrived to make their highest ever total — 705–8 against Surrey, at Hastings. It should have been 1066 really.

There was, however, one county that you will not find in the championship table, either first- or second-class, whose skipper could yet make a run or two. 'London County' was formed by W. G. Grace, passing his final playing days at the old Crystal Palace ground. Since the services of any player in the land could be enlisted at his command, it comes as no surprise that 'The London' were a match for anyone, and attracted a large following. Though the G.O.M. was now well over fifty, that made him no less eager to win, and matches were as keenly fought as if there were points at stake. Yet, even with virtually a Test side on view, the novelty wore thin and, after a brief but gay existence, the club folded through lack of support. As with the Rest of the World team that toured here in 1970, it was found that the public are curiously reluctant to attend friendly matches, however keen the contest. It seems that spectators need to identify with a specific county or country, composite teams are no substitute.

So there was much that was good in the county programme, and let us say that it served to complement rather than rival a most unforgettable Test series, one which was always going to dominate the summer. Of course, it would have been more satisfactory had England won, with the 'right side' being chosen throughout, but perfection in human affairs is a chimera, and should we want it for long if it did materialise?

Had the original team, the Golden Eleven, romped to a 3–0 victory, no doubt there would have been much temporary rejoicing, the selectors voted jolly good chaps, and Fred Tate would have taken late retirement, but should we be writing about it today? I think not. Lord Cardigan's Light Brigade attained immortality not so much for the 'glorious charge they made', as for the fact that the whole business was a colossal and sorry blunder. Similarly, the legend of the brave 300 at Thermopolye is enhanced by the presence of a traitor in their midst.

Such is man's curious preoccupation with human frailty, a frailty that the 1902 season demonstrated with such poignancy. Intrigue and melodrama, mishaps and controversy — they interest the writer because they interest us all.

Yet pleasure, like humour, does not bear too much analysis. Nor, of course, do such judgments do credit to the enthralling cricket played. The plain facts are, that 1902 was a wet, miserable summer that might soon have been forgotten; the momentous happenings of a Test series that was as absorbing as any yet contested, made it a season that lives on to this day. So be it.

It is time to take leave of a world of gaslight and Hansoms; to bid farewell to gaily blazered gods of old, and to seek new vistas amid the playing fields of the mind.

VII – Fight to a Finish

Cricket is not what it used to be. It never was, of course — which might well explain why seasons of the recent past fail to fire the imagination in quite the same way as those of yesteryear. After all, one can hardly have a nostalgic attachment to the happenings of three years ago. Rather like the best pop tunes, they are enjoyed while they are here, then fade quickly into oblivion, only to be revived later as 'golden oldies'. No doubt, given time, the incredible events of 'Botham's Series' in 1981 will fill as many chapters as the scenes we have ourselves described — even though we know that this was the weakest Australian batting side ever to visit these shores, and that Botham's mighty, if still infrequent, exploits apart, much of the cricket was undistinguished. But will that be as obvious in fifty years time?

Again, I am not unmindful of the brilliant and entertaining West Indian teams of the past decade, but it takes two sides to make a memorable series, and England have generally been overwhelmingly outplayed in these contests. Thus, though excellent in themselves, their recent visits have lacked the edge that keener competition might have provided.

However, one could offer less palatable reasons to support my contention that cricket is not what it once was. Granted that time lends enchantment; granted also, that I am an aged buffer inclined to laud the past; but, that said, some things, such as run-and-over-rates do have an objective measure. As statistics prove, the last twenty years has seen a marked decline in the pace at which the game is played and, which is even worse, a tame acceptance of it.

Neither is the present obsession with pace-bowling a figment of the imagination. Speed and seam serve as the staple diet, the new ball a sacred cow, such that — the Asian countries partly excepted — spin-bowling in all its facets is fast becoming a lost art. Variety is forfeited and the over-rate declines. Of nobody is this more true than of the West Indies — by far the strongest team in the world.

Yet not the least disappointing aspect, I fear, is the sub-standard quality of contemporary English teams. Yet, how many top names are competing for places? Our lack of strength-in depth has surely never been more marked. I know one can point to the preponderance of overseas imports to county cricket, or the excess of one-day games, as reasons for this sad state of affairs, but that does not alter the fact that there is more than a hint of pallid mediocrity about the current national side. The great, or even the very good, players are very few indeed, and their number seems to dwindle every year. Perhaps I was spoiled in my youth.

I am not then, you will have gathered, too enamoured of the cricket today. Certainly, I think that much of the gaiety and warmth that went with the feeling that the players were enjoying themselves has gone from the game, though that has much to do with the times we live in. Cricket is not the only sport to be thus afflicted. As for playing strength, all cycles pass and one can only hope for a speedy return to former glories. For the present, one cannot, with the exception of the too-recent 1981 season, recall one year in the last twenty-five that could in any way be called exceptional. Some had their moments, of course, such as the Lord's Test of 1963, but, from an English point of view, that summer is mostly best forgotten. There was some sparkling cricket in 1973 though, again, not too much of it by England, the exhilarating power of the West Indies proving far too much for us.

Who knows how we shall view these years a little while hence? For the moment, however, I am obliged to revert to the mid nineteen-fifties to find an appropriate summer. Here we might pick any one of three.

1956 was, of course, Laker's year, when he, Lock and the peerless Peter May — all of Surrey — were largely responsible for England's successful defence of the Ashes. If we include Surrey's match with the visitors, 'Big Jim' Laker took all ten Australian wickets in an innings, not once, but twice, settling on a third occasion for a mere nine. Lock bowled scarcely less well but enjoyed none of the luck, his one wicket at Old Trafford, against Laker's nineteen, in no way doing him justice. As we have said before, it is the pressure of great bowlers in harness that so often claims wickets — whoever actually takes them. May, as a fairly inexperienced captain, also carried the batting, and, though not without support, was far and away the most consistent batsman throughout.

But ungrateful, not to say perverse, as it may seem to say so, victory here was almost too easy, and what use have such victories ever been to an Englishman? Compared with previous sides, this was an ill-assorted Australian party, few of the old guard remaining, the replacements, for the most part, hardly adequate. Added to which, there were disquieting rumours of collusion, of sub-standard dusty pitches having been expressly prepared for Lock and Laker. And to be honest, from the losers point of view, it did rather look that way. Then again, this was a depressingly wet summer, as films from the BBC archives often show, and all these things together took something of the gilt from the season.

1957, by contrast, though never a 'sizzler', was mainly warm and dry. It also saw the West Indies with their glittering array of talent, including the seventeen-year-old Garfield Sobers, not to mention the 'Spin Twins' — Ramadhin and Valentine. Yet, so strong were England at that time, that, when after a disastrous start defeat looked certain, a magnificent and gargantuan stand of 411 by May and Cowdrey averted it. After this the visitors were fairly trampled underfoot. Though possessed of brilliant individuals, they flattered only to deceive. Having made well over 500 in the first match, West Indies never again threatened to build a big score. England, on the other hand, went from strength to strength. May, Cowdrey and Graveney all made runs; Laker, Lock and Loader — Ls but no learners — largely took the wickets. So again, after that early scare, this was no contest.

Oddly enough too, there was a sense of the inevitable about the county programme, Surrey coasting to their sixth successive championship. It was a marvellous achievement from an extremely strong all-round side. Not only had they the finest county attack seen for many years, plus in Peter May the best batsman to emerge since the war, but they were also a wonderful fielding side close to the wicket. Three players — Stewart, Barrington and Lock — held 204 catches between them, with Stewart's 77 falling just one short of Hammond's 1928 record. But though a good, and in many respects, satisfactory season, the lack of close competition in both Test matches and championships leaves 1957 something short of the best.

More memorable, to my mind, was the long hot summer of 1955. That being so, one wonders why it has been so little written about. Cricket scribes, we know, do not over-concern themselves with the beauties of the weather, but when else, before the disasters of 1984, has a series in this country between major powers seen a result in all five matches? Since India were not considered first-class when losing 5–0 in 1959, the answer is 'never'! Yet England and South Africa managed it here.

Moreover, they conjured a fine series, full of splendid, positive, often exciting, and always entertaining cricket. If Jack Cheetham's side was not the best to visit these islands, they were certainly the fittest. Each morning, before start of play, we were treated to a display of organised gymnastics, as the Springboks went through their work-out. Later, as their efforts bore fruit, one marvelled at their agility in the field; there was always one man covering another, always two in pursuit of the ball.

Yet possibly England had the edge in the close-fielding. Lock was superb anywhere, of course, but particularly 'round the corner', as was Trueman, though he played in only one Test here. Bailey brought off some astonishing catches in the gully, Graveney missed little at slip, while Close, Cowdrey and Ikin were other outstanding close fielders to be depended upon. Yet it must be said that, in one sense, England hardly resembled a *team* at all, looking rather more of a squad. Only four men — May, Compton, Graveney and Bailey — appeared in all five matches and, overall, no fewer than twenty-five players were called upon. It is usually a sign of barrenness when selectors are obliged to make constant changes, but this was a slightly different case. England had returned victorious from Australia only that winter, having retained the Ashes they had regained in 1953. Several younger players had confirmed their promise, and the future augured well. Since then, however, both Hutton and W. J. Edrich had announced their retirement, Hutton's place as an opener, proving particularly difficult to fill, both now and for some time after.

Here, a number of make-shift pairings were tried, none of them proving suitable. For the first three Tests, Graveney was promoted to partner Worcester's Don Kenyon, a player who had been tried before, and who again proved not quite equal to the task. It was also felt that Graveney's fluent stroke-play would be seen to better advantage lower down, and so for Leeds a fresh start was made with Frank Lowson playing on his home ground, and Bailey, who at least would not want for staying power! This again, was something less than successful, and so by the time The Oval Test arrived — having gone through the card as it were — the job was entrusted to Jack Ikin, newly converted by Lancashire to that position, and Close, who was anything but a recognised opener.

Still, there was stability enough in the middle batting, which stayed more-or-less constant, and most of the other changes were attributable to injuries to Evans, behind the stumps, and the bowlers Tyson and Appleyard. Laker did not yet command a regular place, and though it is hard to believe, was brought in only for the final Test, on his home ground. Otherwise, spin was largely the province of the left-armers, Lock and Wardle. In essence then, the England 'side' would normally read something like this: Kenyon, Graveney, May (captain), Compton, A. N. Other, Bailey, Evans, Lock, Wardle, Tyson and Statham. A very fair eleven.

South Africa, as can be the advantage of touring sides, needed to make few changes, their team for the most part picking itself.

Ironically, then, the captain, Cheetham, was forced to miss the third and fourth Tests through injury but, that unfortunate loss apart, their line-up bore a fairly predictable look and, in terms of balance, was perhaps better equipped than most of its predecessors.

In McGlew and Goddard, South Africa had a sound, if unspectacular, opening pair, with Goddard able to operate as a third seamer. Waite, a world-class wicket-keeper, was a good enough batsman to later go in at number three. McLean in full flow offered an exciting prospect; Endean gave solidity to the middle order, while Cheetham could adjust his game to meet any situation. The batting was given further variety by the inclusion of the big-hitting newcomer, Paul Winslow, who came in for three of the matches. A most dangerous player once set, he could see a bowler off in the space of two or three overs. Another newcomer, H. J. Keith, of whom little was known, went in even higher in the order than either Endean or McLean.

The bowling too was well-balanced. Spear-headed by Adcock and Heine, the latter at times produced spells of real pace. At first change, the highly accurate Goddard nagged away with his cutters on a line of leg stump, and got through a lot of work at moderate cost. 'Toey' Tayfield was at this time the best off-spinner extant, and was South Africa's most prolific wicket-taker. Mansell, the leg spinner, was hardly in this class, yet as is the wont of such bowlers, was always likely to take a vital wicket. A useful batsman, he epitomised the modest 'bits and pieces' all-rounder. Fuller, a third new-ball bowler, who came in for two of the Tests, completed the side. Allied to their speed in the field, the side had a solid look to it.

For all that, England were surely favourites. Despite makeshift openers, they looked, man-for-man, to be the stronger eleven. Most of those named for the first Test at Nottingham were fresh from the successful winter tour, though some had little to prove anyway. Compton, though rendered less mobile by his suspect knee, was still very much a Test-class batsman, and what South Africa needed reminding of his passion for their bowling? May, whilst comparatively young and new to the captaincy, had long since affirmed the high promise shown at Charterhouse and elsewhere. Already four years a Test player, with hundreds scored against the best, there was no doubting his pedigree. Bailey too, had been around in top cricket a good while and, currently the world's best all-rounder, was rightly regarded as something of a fixture. Graveney had yet to show the consistency his talents merited, but an excellent Test hundred that winter had given hope of great things to come.

Moreover, on the age-old precept that it is bowlers who win matches, it was here that, Tayfield apart, England seemed to have the heavier artillery. South Africa had no one of Tyson's blistering pace, nor of Statham's testing accuracy. Time and again these two had torn through the Australian batting, and one rather looked for a repeat performance here. Bailey, the third seamer, found more penetration than his opposite number Goddard, yet could still do the same containing job on or outside the leg stump. South Africa certainly had a trump card in Tayfield, with England having no one of a similar type until The Oval Test, but against that, they had only the moderate Mansell to turn the ball from leg, whereas Lock and Wardle were at the head of their trade and complemented each other perfectly. Lock, all bustle and fierce aggression, possessed a 'faster ball'; Wardle, of gentler pace, was more inclined to toss the ball up, and rely on the subtleties of flight, plus a well-disguised 'chinaman'. With players such as Trueman, Loader, Bedser and Laker waiting in the wings, the bowling appeared more than adequate.

Nothing that happened at Trent Bridge gave grounds to alter that belief, nor in any way suggested that England would be greatly extended in the remaining matches. Glorious June weather and a perfect batting wicket made it an ideal toss to win, and May's reign as captain got off to the best of starts. With both openers on trial, and Kenyon particularly anxious to establish himself, England, not unnaturally, went cautiously at the start yet, thereafter, in spite of a fine 81 by May, never at any time threatened to move into top gear. Kenyon, dropped off the fifth ball he received, took four hours over 87, but did enough to earn retention for the next game, yet with the foundations laid, and everyone expecting him to take toll of tired bowling, Compton, inexplicably, allowed himself to be tied down for most of the last session. As so often happens when a batsman starts playing for half-past six, he was out to a timid stroke, with just enough time for England to lose another quick wicket before the close. The feeling was that they had not made the most of a sound start, Compton, the man to whom one looked to exploit such situations, taking most of the blame.

As it happened, it scarcely mattered, England adding enough runs on the second day to make a total that South Africa never looked capable of matching. The only batsman who took the eye did so for the wrong reasons as if wishing to give human form to the virtue of patience. 'Sticker' McGlew certainly lived up to his name, batting on and on in one of the most pugnacious displays ever witnessed in Test cricket. In South Africa's first innings, he stayed 306 minutes for 68, and following on, spent 249 minutes over 51 — a total of nine-and-a-quarter hours at the crease, by which time the England bowlers were heartily tired of him. It may not have been pretty to watch, but as a feat of endurance and concentration performed in the interests of the side, it was deserving of high praise, making the play purposeful and, therefore, interesting. However, even that patient effort could not prevent England winning by an innings and 105 runs, Tyson, as expected, doing most of the damage. On a wicket where Heine and Adcock had been made to look fairly innocuous, Tyson's vital extra pace proved too much for all but McGlew, and a fiery second-innings spell of 6–28 wrapped up the match on the fourth afternoon.

With such a victory — achieved without Hutton or Edrich — England further underlined that the lean years of the post-war era were well and truly over — that the emergence of a side fit to challenge for world supremacy lay not too far off. Apart from the shortage of Test class openers, there was strength-in-depth in all departments, but most significantly, perhaps, came confirmation that at last England possessed a *pair* of fast bowlers with, moreover, ready replacements in Trueman and Loader, should either Tyson or Statham break down.

Tyson's selection for Australia that winter had been seen as something of a gamble but, after cutting down his run following the hard lessons of Brisbane, he fully justified Hutton's faith in speed, he and Statham bowling England to victory in the second and third Tests. Now, on the mildest pitch in England, Tyson had struck again. What might he do on a Lord's wicket that usually gave some assistance to fast bowlers?

Unfortunately, we were not to know. Tyson's proneness to injury in what was a lamentably short international career, put him out of the second match, his replacement, Fred Trueman, despite a sensational debut against India in 1952, had yet to establish a regular place. Two years National Service had retarded his progress, and a stormy tour of the West Indies, where he fell foul of authority, had further prejudiced his chances. Not chosen for the Australian tour, he now had an opportunity to redeem himself.

Indeed, no pace bowler could have wished for a better wicket than that prepared at Lord's that year, it being exceptionally fast, even by normal standards. Winning the toss here had rather less advantage — particularly if the pitch grew slower as the game went on — and May must have viewed his luck as something of a mixed blessing when, after electing to bat, England were shot out for 133. Heine, so ineffective at Trent Bridge, now looked a different bowler. He took 5 for 60 in a really hostile spell and, with more luck, might have produced even better figures.

No score, however, can be properly gauged until both sides have batted, and in truth, had England taken their catches, South Africa would have been dismissed for under a hundred. As it was, McLean, riding his luck — you might say deservedly so — hammered 142 out of 196 in just 105 minutes of glorious stroke-play, enabling South Africa to reach 304. England had cause to regret their lapses in the field. Dropped five times, McLean alone played any sort of an innings on a wicket where most batsmen were beaten for sheer pace. His vastly disproportionate contribution in what looked certain to be a modest scoring match, had ensured a lead of 171 and left his side in a very strong position.

England's long uphill climb began badly when, for the second time in the match, the openers failed to provide a good start. Hopes now of setting their opponents a sizable target in the fourth innings looked decidedly slim; indeed, on the evidence of the match so far, an innings defeat was more than possible. May, however, was at a stage in his career when he consistently made runs in the second innings, and he now proceeded to atone for his first innings failure by producing a faultless hundred of great authority. Without doubt, May still remains the finest batsman to emerge since the war; now, in his first series as captain, he gave further proof of just how aptly that mantle rested upon those slim shoulders. Like Hutton before him, May had not previously lead his county, yet he took the greater responsibility in his stride, his batting both here and at Nottingham apparently unaffected by the onus of leadership. Though quietly spoken, a self-effacing, almost diffident manner off the field, belied a certain belligerence on it — a ruthlessness that one did not quite expect. In fact, he gave little away and lost none of the four series that followed this one. In all, May captained England on a record thirty-eight occasions, and was still only thirty-one when he left cricket for business reasons. What he might have achieved is anyone's guess, but the certainty is, that the commercial world's gain was cricket's loss, for his replacement has been a long time in coming.

Equally deceptive, was the power May generated into strokes played with an easy grace — a calmness born of self-assurance. Though disinclined to hook, he had command of every other stroke, none more so than the straight-and-on-drive in which he excelled. May was at his best when standing up to fast bowlers, when, with steel-like wrists, he cracked the ball past them in almost leisurely fashion. Here, on a fiery Lord's wicket that was too fast for most, May repeatedly drove Heine and Adcock through the narrow arc between long-on and long-off. In a beautiful display of clean hitting, he was unhurried apparently, yet always moving along at a very respectable rate.

Compton too, confirmed that he had lost none of his appetite for South African bowling, keeping May company with a timely innings of 69 that saw him back to something like his best. Together they saw England to relative safety, wiping out the arrears, and providing the foundations of a total that gave the bowlers something to aim at. This was fine cricket for the Saturday crowd; a stand vital to England's chances, was also highly entertaining. In fact, their many attractive partnerships in this series were among the best things on view in the whole summer.

The old and the new. Compton, now that Hutton had departed, the best and very nearly the last of the pre-war greats; May, the brightest star of the new generation. That they were the two finest batsmen in the land, few would contradict, but together, their styles provided ideal foils, each, it seemed, intent on outdoing the other in a medley of varied and delightful strokes. If May crisply bisected the long field, then Compton drove handsomely through the covers; when May turned one sweetly off his legs, Compton responded with a late cut of the utmost delicacy. Stroke-for-stroke they went, and it was some measure of their mastery that they beat the field as often as they did. The brilliance of the South African out-cricket contributed much to the high level of entertainment in this rubber, and only the most perfect placement stood any chance of getting through. As it was, many a thoroughbred stroke brought no runs, as fielders, particularly McGlew in the covers, brought off one stupendous stop after another.

Now, thanks largely to May and Compton, England took their total to 353, but a target of 183, with two days left, did not look too formidable a task for the South Africans. In fact, they got off to the worst of starts. McGlew, their recognised sheet-anchor, and well nigh a fixture at Nottingham, proved rather less troublesome here. Out first ball in the first innings, he improved only slightly on that performance, falling to Statham's second delivery, and bagging a pair. South Africa were at once struggling and though the next wicket or two offered brief resistance, Statham, bowling unchanged from the start, ripped through the innings in mid-afternoon to finish with 7–39 from 29 overs. England were home by 71 runs, and had again seen off their opponents inside four days.

No one at this stage would have given much for South Africa's chances of squaring the series, or even, perhaps, of winning a match.

Two down with three to play, their plight was further worsened by an injury to Cheetham which was to put him out of the next two Tests. Indeed, any faint hope of a come-back appeared to have vanished altogether when, on a beautiful Old Trafford wicket, May won the toss for the third time in a row. This was the best pitch produced that summer — the ideal cricket wicket — fast and true, yet of even bounce. Batsmen could play their strokes; bowlers were not without hope. Fluent stroke-makers like May, Compton and Graveney would surely put the match, and the rubber, beyond South Africa's reach. So much for theory.

England made several changes for this game, though one, the return of the now fit Tyson, was wholly predictable. As luck would have it, however, his partner Statham, the hero of Lords, was himself forced to drop out, so the jinx which, after the first Test, prevented this pair from taking the field together, had struck once more. In the event, the selectors brought in Bedser and left out Trueman. This was difficult to understand. Trueman had done nothing wrong at Lords, giving Statham sound support, and picking up a few wickets himself. Moreover, he was young, fast, a prospect for the future, and more likely to extract something from this wicket than would a medium-pacer.

Bedser, on the other hand, for so long England's main, and at times only strike bowler, had suffered a bitter disappointment in Australia that winter. Following a listless performance at Brisbane, when still weak from the effects of shingles, he was discarded for the next match, and subsequently found no place in Hutton's speed strategy — apparently a sad climax to a fine Test career, in which he had literally bowled his heart out. Now, at thirty-seven, he was brought back and one must ask: Was this fair or, indeed, necessary? If he was considered back to his best, why had he not played at Lords, on a wicket that gave maximum assistance? The truth was that, not unnaturally at that age and afters years spent bowling himself into the ground, Bedser as a Test match bowler was now in decline. The renowned zip off the pitch that made him something more than medium-paced, had faded. He was still a very good bowler, but no longer a great one. Was it likely, then, that Bedser would get more out of this wicket than either Trueman or Loader?

Another change was to bring in Cowdrey for Barrington, whose Test baptism in the two matches so far had hardly been a success. In fairness, he could be counted unlucky in that his only innings at Nottingham had started at a quarter-past six when the light was at its worst, while the fast Lord's wicket had had almost everyone in trouble. Yet it was some time before this solid, gritty player was given another chance to establish himself as the automatic choice we came to know.

Cowdrey, who like May, had shown considerable promise from early schooldays, and of whom great things were expected, had hitherto, for sundry reasons, missed out on selection this season. One of the finds of the Australian tour, and hailed as the new Hammond, one had assumed that his place was now more or less assured. However, the Government, and more particularly H.M. Forces, waits neither for man nor cricketer and, on return, Cowdrey was duly called up for National Service. And there his troubles began. Found to have bad feet, he failed the medical. For anybody else, that would have been the end of the matter. Not for Cowdrey. There is always an element only too ready to throw stones, and the cynics were quick to assert that anyone who could play cricket six days a week, had nothing much wrong with his feet — in short, that Cowdrey had somehow pulled strings to get out of his two-year stint. It was nonsense, of course, and malicious nonsense at that. We should know that Colin Cowdrey was never a man to shirk anything. Did he not a year hence, without reservation or public statement, take on the unsought opener's job and, thereafter, shuttle up and down the order to meet the needs of the side? Did he not take over the captaincy in mid-series when May was indisposed? Was he not twice — in 1965 and 1974 — rushed out in mid-winter as replacement for depleted touring sides, and did he not, at Lords in 1963, with broken arm, go out to face the wrath of Hall and Griffiths to ensure a famous draw?

Nevertheless, much was made of it, and with having to face R.A.F. Boards, and still being up at Oxford, Cowdrey played only limited cricket this season. That at 22, and the subject of a hurtful smear campaign, he could keep his mind on cricket at all, let alone undergo the searching examination of a Test match, tells something not only of his class, but also of his mettle as a man. Time and again, he was to be dropped or passed over for the captaincy, often by men not his equal, yet never with one word of dissent. Nor would one have expected otherwise. A devout churchman of deep convictions and great personal courage,* Cowdrey wisely preferred to let his bat do the talking. His conduct on the field was exemplary too. If he claimed a catch, you were sure to be out, and his sporting inclination to 'walk' became a by-word. As a cricketer, his 8,000 runs and 100 catches in Test cricket speak for

---

*Cowdrey is one of three players — the Rev. David Sheppard and Rev. Congdon are the others — to have scored a Test century on a Saturday, and read the lesson on Sunday, he and Congdon both being lay-preachers.

themselves. As a man, though at times hurt as few men have been, Cowdrey showed himself to be cut from whole cloth.

His belated presence now added one more fluent stylist to England's attractive batting line-up, and it was hard to imagine that such a wealth of assorted talent could fail. Yet fail it did — with one exception. Compton, who had always shown a liking for Manchester, played a typical saving innings to be 155 not out at the close, but a total of little over 250 for the loss of eight wickets said little for the rest.

Hopes that the following morning might see Compton and the tail add another 50 runs or so were short-lived. Yesterday's hero added only three more to his overnight score, and the innings ended at 284. It seemed a most unsatisfactory total in the circumstances, and, as if to prove it so, South Africa went easily along to 147–1 before McGlew was forced to retire with a damaged hand. This opened the way for a mini-collapse. Yet, at 245 for five, with Waite still there, and looking in good order, together with the prospect of McGlew's return, there was still every chance that they would overtake England's total.

In glorious, warm June sunshine, jokes about Manchester weather were silenced as South Africa set about first repairing, then consolidating their innings. It was in the afternoon that the fireworks really began. Until then, with Waite leading the way, they had attempted little more than to ensure a healthy first innings lead. Now the big-hitting Winslow, who could never restrain himself for long, decided that this was the moment to open up.

To see him at the crease, rimless spectacles glinting in the sunlight, one would not at once have identified him as a player who hit sixes for a pastime. A court of law seemed a more natural setting for this unassuming, studious-looking young man. In fact, Winslow was an active volcano, likely at any time to erupt. He might play three or four balls sedately back along the pitch, only to nonchalantly lift the next two, apparently identical, deliveries, far into the crowd. Such latent power gave the bowler no advance warning of the big hit; there was no leap to meet him, no elaborate wind-up — just a last-minute acceleration of the down-stroke, as with a lazy swing he hit the ball on the up, still from the crease. One could only sense, as now, when the volcano was about to burst forth.

To have seen Winslow's innings that day, would have been sufficient in itself. There have been faster, more frenzied innings, but as a display of controlled aggression, this made a marvellous sight. Before one quite realised it, he had slammed his way to 108, yet at no time did he give the impression of making a non-stop onslaught, still less that each attempted six-hit would be his last. This was not slogging; he simply picked the ball to hit and chose correctly. So correctly, in fact, that he reached his hundred with one of the biggest hits that Cowdrey for one, claims he has ever seen. Like other long hitters, he was a genuine batsman first, though perhaps lacking the all-round technique to be as consistent as he would have wished. Apart from two matches in 1949, Winslow figured but briefly in Test cricket, and this was his only visit to these shores. How glad we were that he had left us something to remember.   `

Waite meanwhile, had not been idle, and the two put on 171 for the fifth wicket, a record in these matches. Waite made 123. This was a fine innings, though inevitably overshadowed by Winslow's pyrotechnics. A very correct player, he brought the same cultured look to his batting as he displayed behind the stumps — a most polished performer. At 457-7, McGlew, after a weekend's rest, returned to complete an unbeaten one hundred and four, before declaring on Monday morning at 521-8.

South Africa had a lead of 237. Barring a cricket miracle — and there have been quite a few — there could be only two results; a victory for McGlew's men that would keep the rubber alive, but a draw would leave South Africa dormy two. If the first were to be avoided, England would have to bat somewhat better than they had done on Thursday.

This appeared to be no more than wishful thinking when both openers were dismissed with only two on the board. 2-2! May, however, again saved his best for the second innings, and now, with the evergreen Compton, went some way to retrieving the situation. Compton, though, batting even better than he had done in the first innings, was, if anything, the more prominent of the two. In his most carefree vein, he reached 71 with strokes that were in vintage vein, and little seemed more certain than that he would go on to his second century of the match. But then, as often happens, a bowling change brought about his downfall, Heine inducing an edge with the first ball of a new spell.

May suffered only slightly by comparison, and he too was looking odds-on a century maker. He was now joined by Cowdrey, playing his first Test in England, and a man fortified to play a long innings, if ever there was one. A healthy eater, that growing lad had managed a breakfast of cereal, eggs and bacon, three trout, toast and marmalade. No doubt the R.A.F. were relieved to be spared the cost of feeding him. More seriously, Cowdrey has stated that, his own poor form aside, this was one of the best Tests he ever played in. He was the last person to make excuses for himself, yet it is hard to believe that the many abusive letters Cowdrey received in the course of this summer had not sorely distressed him. As ever, he kept a discreet silence, but one thinks that the pressure must to some extent have affected him.

He was not helped by the position confronting him. Necessary as runs were, it was more important to stay there. Even if, as now seemed likely, England averted the innings defeat, they would still be hard pressed to set the South Africans a target much in excess of 150, which, with time on their side, they might be expected to reach comfortably. With the weather set fair, England would have to bat out the rest of Monday and through most of Tuesday if they were to commit their opponents to a run chase. How best to approach their task?

Clearly a great deal depended on May and Cowdrey, the two best products of the post-war era, but while May bristled with the confidence that comes with success, Cowdrey, feeling the lash of public opinion, was struggling to find his best form. Not that the open-minded saw him as anything other than a victim of circumstance, and at least as many sympathetic cheers as predictably ill-becoming cat-calls accompanied his progress to the crease. He was, after all, playing for England, and England had great need of an innings from him now.

In one sense, and that perhaps the most important, Cowdrey did no less than was asked of him. Though plainly out of touch and finding it difficult to get the ball away, he gave solid support of his captain, and was still there at the close. He would fight another day. May reached the hundred that had always looked inevitable, but at 114 was surprisingly deceived by a gentle leg-break from Mansell that disturbed the top of his stumps. Though by no means out of the wood, England had at least virtually ensured that South Africa would have to bat again, and with the wicket at the end of the fourth day beginning to show signs of wear, there was hope that we might yet be in for an interesting finish.

Of course, the odds still very much favoured South Africa — the more so in view of doubts concerning Evans's fitness. He had injured a hand during South Africa's long innings, and the extent of the damage was not quite known. At length, it was somewhat euphemistically announced that he would bat 'if needed'. He would, however, be unable to keep wicket, that task falling to Graveny. Poor Tom. This was not his match. Having failed twice with the bat and put down two catches at slip, he was now asked to step into the unaccustomed, and highly-specialised role of wicket keeper — on a wearing wicket. Keeping to Tyson could not have been what he most wanted in life and, gallantly as Graveney performed, he was obliged to stand so far back that, before the end, the batsmen were running byes to him!

Thus, although only four wickets were down, England's batting thereafter was rather an unknown quantity. Cowdrey and Bailey might be relied upon but, without the lively Evans, the 'fifty-makers' really ended at six. Titmus, it was true, was played as an all-rounder, but this was only his second Test, and as yet he had done little with either bat or ball. Lock, Tyson and Bedser were, of course, no tyros, but, in essence, the next wicket would see one end open. So, much rested on Cowdrey and Bailey.

England duly edged ahead, but they had still a long way to go if South Africa were to be pushed to a run chase. Occupation of the crease had to be the first priority. To that end, Crowdrey's long fight, not only against the bowlers, but with his own patchy form, has to be seen as invaluable. Since his off-side play had attracted comparison with the great Walter Hammond, it was not the innings it might have been. Certainly, he himself took small satisfaction. Nevertheless, in dallying for more than four hours over his 54 runs, Cowdrey brought England that much nearer to saving the match.

Bailey, who seemed to revel in this sort of situation, was now England's main hope. Not for the first time in recent years, he applied himself only to survival, the forward push, head right over the ball, his stock-in-trade. Unflappable in crisis, Bailey's powers of concentration were legion, disheartening for bowlers, but immensely reassuring to English morale. Even so, wickets fell steadily at the other end, and by mid-afternoon, with nine wickets down, the lead was a precarious one of under a hundred. About three hours remained.

Evans, as announced, now joined Bailey. With the injured man prepared to bat virtually one-handed in order to use up precious time, and with Tayfield bowling, McGlew might have reverted to his quick bowlers. In fact, he persevered with the spinner. This was not, I think, in deference to Evans's plight. Sportsman that he was, McGlew's first duty was to win the match and so keep the rubber alive. Having come this close, he was not likely to allow finer feelings to override his judgment. England would not have wished him to. No, he probably reasoned that an incapacitated batsman would have problems against the turning ball, while, simply by offering a straight bat, he might edge or glance fours off the faster bowlers.

Whatever the logic of this reasoning, Evans confounded it. So far from prodding tentatively forward, he set out to attack Tayfield from the start and, largely with the one good hand, hit hard, high and often into the long-field, not, it is true, always cleanly, or with precise aim, but certainly with infinite resolve. In no time he had reached 30, and McGlew was now faced with a tricky decision. Tea was at hand; England were almost 140 runs on, and two more overs of Evans in this form would begin to make South Africa's task look daunting. Yet the spinners were more likely to induce the mis-hit. He decided to give Tayfield one more over.

Two clubbing blows took Evans to 36. McGlew looked a worried man. Tayfield too wore an air of disbelief. He had not strayed from line or length, and on another day might have had Evans caught more than once. But this was not his day; by luck or judgment, the lofted stroke landed safely time and again between the fielders, at times tantalisingly so. What to do? Tayfield tossed up yet another impeccable delivery, and this time Evans struck what was an enormous blow for one so incapacitated. It soared pavilionwards, but with too much height, and insufficient length, and McLean, lurking in the deep, was fast making ground for the catch.

For what seemed an age, all held their breath as the ball hovered, the hopes of two nations resting with it. Would the ball fall short; would the fielder stay calm? These are nasty catches at the best of times; now, with the match delicately poised, having to take such a catch in front of the pavilion with the crowd, or most of it, silently willing you to drop it, was a test for the strongest nerve. McLean, in this hot summer, had a heavy tan, yet was it only imagination that he paled beneath it, as, head craned, he clutched the ball gratefully to his chest?

It was a noble end to a gallant innings, one which had not quite swung the game, but had certainly contrived to make it interesting. England's total of 388 now left South Africa wanting 145 runs to win, with, in all, 132 minutes in which to make them. The target seemed reasonably straightforward, although the need to keep the score moving, with its attendant risk of losing wickets, gave England some cause for hope.

Somewhat against their nature, McGlew and Goddard went on the attack from the start, but soon Goddard was caught by May off Bedser for 8. 18 for one. When, soon after Keith was clean-bowled by Bedser without scoring, South Africa were suddenly in trouble at 23 for two. But McLean, coming in next, immediately spelt danger for England. Essentially an attacking player, this was in many ways a situation made for him, but it must be said that Tyson, always the most menacing of the England bowlers, made life fairly easy for him by pitching too short, too often. Hooking and cutting magnificently, McLean lashed his way to 50 in 50 minutes, and at 95 for two, the match looked as good as won.

McGlew, almost forgotten in our dismay over the carnage taking place at the other end, was going along steadily, sound in defence, yet losing no opportunity to score, and neither batsman appeared in any kind of trouble. There seemed no danger either when McLean cut hard to backward point, where the ball was half stopped before running on beyond the fielder. But the batsmen started out, hesitated, and then went again and, with the ball being quickly retrieved and thrown in, McLean was caught well out of his ground. 95 for three. One major threat had been removed, but another now came in the form of Winslow, sent in ahead of Endean.

Since Winslow's intentions could easily be guessed, May, with few runs to play with, was faced with a problem similar to the one Evans had earlier set McGlew. Did one use speed or spin? Tyson, certainly, would afford little scope for the straight hit, but he was being rested and, in any case, could not bowl at both ends. Yet almost every other option involved risk. Off-spinner Titmus had not the experience at this level, and had so far proved expensive. Lock too, had known better matches, while medium-pace seam on this wicket was apple-pie to a hitter. Nevertheless, with limited options, May decided to bring back the old war-horse, Bedser, the only bowler thus far to have taken a wicket. Even at medium-pace, Bedser's control of line and length, plus his ability to move the ball both ways, might prove Winslow's undoing. In the past it had often undone no less a batsman than Bradman.

But bowling to a man who scorns orthodoxy is never easy, especially when runs are at a premium. One felt for Bedser, and prayed that May's decision would not prove ill-judged. Winslow, however, confirmed our worst fears, hoisting Bedser for a huge six in his first over, and striking him for another a few balls later. He reached 16 in no time, leaving only 33 more runs to be made. This could not go on. May quickly brought back Tyson, and was immediately rewarded with the sight of Winslow's off-stump cartwheeling out of the ground. Much relief. 112 for four. Yet one still regretted the precious runs lost in a few brief minutes.

The hitters were gone, but South Africa still had plenty of batting in hand, and they were well up with the clock. McGlew was now leading the way, and looking as solid as ever. He had made over 40, and one felt that while he was there, South Africa must prevail. If, on the other hand, he should be dismissed, England might yet have a faint chance.

Imagine the delight then, when Tyson, now at a furious pace, uprooted McGlew's off stump before he had properly fashioned a stroke — the second occurrence within a few minutes of this most thrilling of sights, 129 for five. The anchor man gone. Yet, with just 16 runs wanted, the bowlers had, one thought, too little room for error.

Three runs later, Tyson struck again, having Mansell leg before wicket with a thunderous delivery. With signs of nerves creeping in, so now did the fielders. Endean, confronted with a ring of close-catchers, duly found the hands of one of them with a tentative push at Lock. 135 for seven. Could England yet snatch victory? No. For all their pressure, no further wicket fell, and Waite with 10 not out, steered South Africa home with three wickets, nine balls, five minutes, but absolutely no nervous energy, to spare.

Despite making their task unnecessarily difficult, South Africa were back in the rubber and deservedly so. Batting second, they made better use of a good wicket, and succeeded in bowling England out twice. In Cheetham's absence, McGlew had led the side shrewdly and well, not least by the example he set with the bat. They would make few changes for Leeds.

For England though, the match exposed several deficiencies and, while the problem of openers had no obvious solution, it was clear that, both there and elsewhere, changes would have to be made. Since making 91 together in the first Test, Kenyon and Graveney had opened together in four innings, and failed to reach double figures on each occasion. Graveney, as one with no pretensions to opening, could be easily excused. In any case, as a graceful stroke-maker he could now attempt to fulfill his undoubted potential in a more suitable middle-order position. The same, alas, could not be said for Kenyon. Much like Fred Tate, he proved an excellent county player who yet fell just short of the highest class. Year in, year out, Kenyon made his 2,000 runs for Worcester, yet in eight Tests, over three series, he had never looked convincing. Clearly his chance had come and gone. Cricket knows many disappointments, not many of them, thankfully, as traumatic as Fred Tate's.

Yet, who would be his replacement? In the end, the selectors went for Frank Lowson, Hutton's protégé, who would at least have the benefit of playing in front of a home crowd. He was another receiving a second chance, though, in all honesty, he looked a less likely prospect than Kenyon, who had the far more consistent county record. Acclaimed as a new find in 1951, Lowson's promise had never quite developed, and his playing days were relatively soon over. To further underline the desperate shortage of Test-class openers at this time, Bailey was chosen as his partner.

This was extraordinary in the light of England's rich array of talent in other positions, and shows just how much England owed to the Hutton-Washbrook partnership in the immediate post-war years. During that time, only Reg Simpson came anywhere near to being an adequate replacement, and not until the arrival of Peter Richardson, in 1956, was the void left by their departure in part overcome. Even then, England had to resort to Cowdrey in order to light on a regular pairing.

Bailey's elevation countered one problem but created another. His was a very special role since his presence at six gave the side balance. The steadying influence when things when wrong, he was the best of all men in a crisis. Some went so far as to say that if there were no crisis when Bailey went in, then he would soon invent one of his own, but that, perhaps was a rather harsh judgment on a player whose obdurate batting had done so much to help regain the Ashes in 1953. The fact remained, that with Graveney back at five, the side was well-stocked with potential run makers, but lacked a sheet-anchor in the event of early disasters. They would not find anyone quite like Bailey, of course, and had Cowdrey not injured a finger, he would have made the sixth batsman. The next batsman to be called up, Willie Watson, also had to cry off, and the job finally went to Doug Insole, who, it would be fair to say, was better appreciated for his ability to graft than for a propensity to entertain. In fact, the nearest they might get to Bailey.

Titmus was another who felt the axe, though, at only twenty-two, his turn would come again. A cheerful, honest cricketer, he himself was ruefully aware that after two Tests, bowling figures of 1–101 and a batting average of nine, hardly argued for his retention. Rather than replace him with another off-spinner, however, they opted to play the two left-armers, Lock and Wardle. With Statham now back, there was predictably no place for Bedser, and the other two changes were enforced, Loader coming in for the injured Tyson, and a third Surrey player, Arthur McIntyre, replacing Evans behind the stumps. With no detriment to the replacements, the side was plainly weakened by the loss of three first-choice players.

As if to reward South Africa's gallant fight back, McGlew at last won the toss. Not that this seemed to have done them much good, when, on what looked to be a good Leeds wicket, they found themselves at 38–5, and in disarray. At this stage, with Statham and Loader bowling superbly, there seemed every prospect of their being bowled out for less than three figures, yet in the afternoon, thanks largely to McGlew and Endean, they recovered — or rather, were allowed to recover — to the almost respectable heights of 171.

England fared little better. After another poor start — both openers out with only twenty on the board, some fine attractive batting by May and Compton gave the innings some substance, but, thereafter, the rest quickly succumbed to Heine. In restricting England to a lead of just twenty, which seemed a poor safeguard for a team having to bat last, Heine can surely have bowled no faster that year. Indeed, Insole, who in a stay of an hour managed just three singles out of 39 runs scored, said that he had never faced more hostile bowling. He found it almost impossible to get the ball away, adding wryly that he almost wished he had been out for a well-played nought, rather than suffer the frustration of constant playing and missing. We know well what he meant.

South Africa did much better when they went in again, McGlew (133) and Goddard (74) putting on 174 for the first wicket. Endean then weighed in with an unbeaten 116, and at tea on the fourth day, the innings closed at exactly 500. Wardle was quite the best of the England bowlers, figures of four for 100 in 57 overs, in a large total representing a fine, sustained piece of spin-bowling.

England required 481 to win in 500 minutes or, perhaps more realistically, needed to bat out two hours and twenty minutes that night and all of the next day in order to save the match. After two days in the field, playing through the last session is never a pleasant prospect; an inexperienced opening pair with one half of it fighting for his place, were not going to lead off at a gallop. Also, there was news that the wear and tear on Compton's knee made it inadvisable for him to bat that night, not, of course, that we hoped he would need to. It was doubly important, then, for Lowson and Bailey to entrench with runs at this stage of secondary importance. With a sound start, the situation could be reviewed in the morning.

Lowson, however, was dismissed for only three, his second failure of the match marking the end of his Test career. This brought in May, who once again put the innings back on course, and at the close England were 115 for two, with Insole, sent in ahead of Compton, 30 not out.

On the last day, England needed 366 to win at a rate of a run a minute, a tall order for any side. The 1948 Australians may have made 404 in a day, but they were rather special. Yet here the orders were that England were to go for the runs. With hindsight, being 2–1 up in the series, it might have been more prudent to play for the draw, but it is a moot point whether over-obsession with defence, which tends to hand the initiative to the bowlers, offers any more chance of batting out a whole day. Stroke-makers are happier playing their natural game, and an offensive approach, while using up precious time as the ball is retrieved, also ensures that your opponents cannot afford to set a too-attacking field. Best of all, of course, it is more entertaining for the spectator.

Each case must be judged on its merits, however, and, of the England sides to take the field this summer, this was probably the least well-equipped to embark on a prolonged run chase. A target of almost 500 required that two batsmen played big innings, and only three — May, Compton and Graveney — could be fancied to do so at the required rate. With one not fully fit, this was asking a good deal. A side that contained a fair share of limited grafters might have been better served by a less ambitious aim. But then, we all know the right tactics from the stand.

Clearly, if England were to win this match, a steady rate of scoring would have to be established and maintained, yet, with two wickets already down, it was essential to get a good start. Thus they faced something of a dilemma from the outset, and their task was made yet more difficult by South Africa's defensive, but entirely justifiable, bowling tactics. Goddard's true merit was always in containment, rather than penetration, and now, with that familiar nagging attack on or outside leg-stump, he restricted England to 45 runs in seventy-five minutes. His methods paid a double dividend when he induced Insole, just short of his fifty, and conscious of falling behind the clock, into attempting to swing him away. The catch at leg slip made England 160 for three.

Compton, his knee heavily strapped, now came in to join May, and immediately began playing his strokes. May had played quite beautifully from the start and there was a time in the hour before lunch when the two, scoring off almost every ball, looked to have put England on a much truer course. However, Compton's delightful innings was all too brief, and, even worse, May was dismissed shortly before the interval, just three short of his hundred.

With hope of winning now effectively gone, England's remaining batsmen were obliged to concentrate on saving the match. They never looked capable of doing so. Wickets fell steadily throughout the afternoon, and, shortly after tea, England were all out for a disappointing 256. Even though the task should probably have never been attempted, it was still desperately disappointing, after May's fine lead, to lose by as many as 224 runs.

South Africa, on the other hand, had every reason to be jubilant. On their knees on the first morning, and seemingly out of contention at 38–5, they had again fought back magnificently under McGlew's leadership, the margin of victory this time leaving no room for doubt. The series was now wide open, and only a brave man would bet confidently on the outcome. Hopes, with some justification, ran high in a rejuvenated Springbok camp.

Although England could point to the fact that they had been forced to put out a weakened side, the feeling was that, twice now, they had thrown matches away, and with them, possibly, the rubber. Psychologically, England were very much in a trough, each result having grown progressively worse — from overwhelming superiority at Nottingham, to inglorious defeat at Leeds. The cohesion of the side had, of course, been affected by injuries, yet it was worrying to see too much responsibility continually placed upon the same few players. May and Compton consistently carried the batting; Statham, and Tyson, when he played, were the match-winning bowlers. Bailey, in this specialist role, had no superior or even equal; nor of course had Evans, whose presence at Leeds was sorely missed — not least for his batting. Others, such as Wardle, had had their moments, but the general impression was that England were not, in the best sense of the word, at team.

The make-shift eleven for the fourth Test would have shown changes anyway; the need for these, in the light of the overall performance, was now even more marked. For so important a match as now promised for The Oval, it was crucial to field the strongest side available, even if, with Evans, Tyson and Cowdrey nursing injuries, it could not be the best. In fact, Tyson was missed less than he might have been. Although, in marked contrast to earlier days, the Oval was now predominantly a bowler's pitch, it tended to favour spin and seam rather than speed. Since Tyson's greatest asset lay in his sheer pace, England were perhaps better served by having just Statham and Bailey to share the new ball. This left room for two spinners, the selectors, on the sound principle of 'horses for courses', putting their faith in the Surrey masters, Laker and Lock. On the equally sound principle, that, on a helpful wicket, four main bowlers will usually achieve no less than would five, the selectors preferred the insurance of an extra batsman.

Few, I think, would doubt the wisdom of these judgments. The attack, fairly well, took care of itself. In the main it was not the bowling that had failed England this summer, but rather the inconsistency in the batting. Here, the selectors deserved some sympathy. True, they were no nearer to resolving the problem of openers, yet several candidates had been tried, and the cupboard was bare — something they would have to live with for a while. But, apart from at Leeds, they had chosen sides which, on paper, had looked capable of scoring far more runs than they had done. Unluckily, though, none of their experiments — Barrington, Titmus, Kenyon, Lowson — had come off; Cowdrey, the one new player who would have made a difference, was effectively denied to them, while Graveney's infuriating inability to produce his best form in Test matches was an enigma that exasperated all. Yet, as a class player of high promise, he had to play. So, although in theory there was no shortage of batting talent, in practice, the selectors had little room for manoeuvre.

May, Compton and Bailey picked themselves, and, together with Graveney, accounted for four of the batting places. That left them to find an opening pair and a seventh batsman as proof against the wicket. An original choice at Leeds, Watson was the natural selection for the latter spot, but to whom did one turn to see the shine off the new ball? Bailey, as we had hoped, now reverted to his old position, and Lowson had again proved out of his depth. Fast running out of ideas, it seemed, they chose the unlikely pairing of Brian Close and Jack Ikin, of whom only Ikin played in that position for his county. Still, one felt they could hardly do worse than their predecessors.

In the continued absence of Evans, a wicket-keeper who could also bat was sought to replace McIntyre, whose recall to Headingley had not been a happy one. In the end, Dick Spooner, who went in high up the order for Warwickshire, won the selectors' vote. Thus the team batted down to number eight, and seemed as good a combination as could be found for this match and on this wicket.

South Africa had selection problems of a different kind — who to leave out now that Cheetham was back after injury. Well as the team had performed in his absence, someone, unless it was the captain himself, would have to be left out. Winslow, in fact was the unlucky omission, a decision which cannot have been taken lightly. South Africa, no doubt, like England, wanted all the batting possible, and must have seen a hitter such as Winslow as something of a risk on a wicket that was certain to take spin. He either came off or did not, and, against the turning ball, the margin of error was that much finer. It was probably a sounder policy to retain their orthodox batsmen, though the decision, as we say, must have been an agonising one.

That apart, South Africa's team was much as expected, less strong, man for man, than England's, possibly, but collectively much on a par. If they had no one quite in the class of May and Compton, South Africa's out-cricket was worth a good fifty runs, and they were, above all, a *team* — a team that had grown in stature as the summer wore on.

As the score in the rubber indicated, the balance was now a fine one.

Never before had two sides come to The Oval level at two matches apiece, and that factor alone guaranteed a sell-out. There was a Saturday start for this fifth and deciding match, when ironically, for the first time that summer, half a day's play was lost to rain, a thunderstorm flooding the ground in mid-afternoon. However, it was that good old-fashioned summer downpour that falls heavily but not at great length and, thereafter, the match was played in gloriously hot weather.

Whatever Cheetham's merits as a Test skipper, he must certainly go down as an unlucky one. Having twice lost the toss, and then missed the next two games as McGlew managed to turn the tide, he now returned to call incorrectly yet again, thus surrendering first innings to England. Yet that appeared to be no bad thing, when after Saturday's rain, England were all out by Monday lunchtime for a mere 151, Goddard taking five for 31. Ironically, Ikin and Close had given them their best start, 51, since Trent Bridge, but, apart from Close, only Compton reached 30. All this, however, had to be seen in perspective. On a drying pitch, and this one in particular, 200 might take some getting; an innings of 30 or 40, in relative terms, could be worth many a hundred. Even so, it did seem that England had hardly taken full advantage of winning the toss.

As one might expect after the morning's tumble of wickets, South Africa began their innings with obvious distrust of the pitch, McGlew and Goddard intent mainly on survival, content if they could to weather the first hour. In theory, the hot sun should have dried out the wicket, making it less variable. Normally then, buying time would have given a better chance to those batsmen to come, but if it was ever in their minds that conditions would grow progressively easier, they were sadly in error. With rain or not, this wicket had a reputation for turning almost from first to last, and justification of it was not long in coming.

England began with Statham and Bailey, with Bailey soon striking the first crucial blow, removing Goodard for eight. But, after just five overs of each, May, who was captaining the side on his home ground, was able to turn to his two foremost county spinners. Although not Surrey's captain, May's day to day acquaintance with Lock and Laker ensured he would get the best out of them. Laker, for instance, preferred to be bowled in long spells; he needed time to settle into a groove. It was safe to assume, therefore, that he was now due for a fairly lengthy stint.

It was interesting to compare the approach of these two great Surrey spinners. Lock was all bustle and belligerence — always in a hurry to bowl, never allowing the batsman time to settle. Here was naked aggression, calculated to intimidate, each stentorian appeal positively demanding a wicket. There was nothing very genial, or genteel, about 'Lockie'.

At the other end was Laker — impassive, inscrutable. One can still picture the almost resigned air with which he slowly wheeled at the end of his walk-back, before ambling in to deliver with his high, easy economical action. You felt no great sense of expectancy as Laker prepared to bowl; he showed none of the venom that promised a wicket with every ball. For all his rare ability to run through sides, he never gave the impression of being impatient to get at batsmen. Even when, a year later, Laker was bowling himself to immortality at Old Trafford, there was no especial eagerness in his step, no suggestion that he was anxious to finish things off. Just the same nonchalant shuffle to the wicket, his polite enquiries those of a man assured of the outcome. Wickets fell to Laker, it seemed, inevitably and painlessly. Though he might beat the bat with indecent regularity, he did not, from the stand *look* a dangerous bowler. From the batsman's point of view, it was all, no doubt, rather different.

In fact, it was Lock who struck first, and decisively, clean bowling Keith for five, having Endean caught without scoring, and then bowling McLean for one; South Africa were 33 for four before he had broken sweat. This sensational start, fully endorsed the claims made about the wicket. By comparison, Laker, as he quietly dropped into a rhythm, looked nothing like as dangerous, but then this was Laker — wheeling away at his trade, unhurried as, like a hypnotist, he first lulled, then mesmerised batsmen into playing the stroke he compelled. Hence his desire to be given a long bowl. Hence also the deadliness of his combination with Lock. Subtlety so well complimented aggression. With pressure at both ends, batsmen found it a case of the frying pan or the fire. To escape the one, only to be confronted with the other, proved no great blessing. It mattered not who took the wickets.

For the moment, though, further success was denied them, as McGlew and Waite set about repairing the wreckage. The trouble with a flurry of wickets is that it makes one hungry for more, and any sort of stand thereafter leads to irrational impatience. Twenty runs without a breakthrough, and it almost seems as if the game is slipping away. It was so here. Of all the Springboks, McGlew was the hardest to remove and Waite, as he had shown at Old Trafford, had a cool head in a crisis. Slowly, ten, twenty, thirty they added, and with 70 on the board, and tea approaching, were still together. Laker allowed them barely more than a run an over for the connoisseur, wholly understandable and admirable; for the partisan, spoiled by the earlier dramatics, most frustrating.

However, one had to be satisfied with the outcome overall, and, at tea, the general view of those near me was that England would have done very well if, by the close, they had seven down for about 130. Caught up in the friendly atmosphere that prevailed at these matches, I found myself entering a 'sweepstake' on what the actual score would be. Deciding that, amongst total strangers (though extremely good-natured ones) I should in no way appear a 'wet blanket', I waived my natural caution and ventured a forecast of 115 for seven — the most hopeful put forward, and one which I thought, privately, seemed to ask a good deal.

Now, as we moved into the last session, England, in need of an early break-through, began with Statham and Laker, speed and spin. Despite the fact that England had come into the match with only four main bowlers, Statham's chief function here was to relieve the spinners — rather than the other way about — while Bailey bowled only eleven overs in the match, further proof of the nature of the wicket. However, the ploy paid off now, Statham claiming the priceless wicket of McGlew, caught behind for 30. 77 for five. Barely had we partisans got over our jubilation at removing that particular thorn than Laker, thinking it high time that he got in on the act, had Waite caught by Lock at short-leg.

Six down and the score not yet eighty; with time in hand, my 'bet' was looking good. "I said six," chuckled one of the syndicate, "But I hope I'm wrong!"

"I said 135 for seven," chipped in another, "Yet I think our friend here will be nearer the mark," and handed me a bottle of beer — though whether this was by way of premature 'prize' or just plain esprit de corps, I could not say.

Lock was now back in the attack, but it was Laker who at length made me a winner, trapping Mansell leg before wicket for six. 86 for seven. They would be lucky to reach 120 at this rate. Cheetham was the last of the recognised batsmen, and he was not over-working the scorers. However, with Tayfield offering a straight bat to the spinners, the score crept past ninety, and again we became impatient for a wicket. Back came Statham for a final burst and not even the straightest of bats prevented Tayfield's castle tumbling. 91 for eight. "Well we're all wrong," I voiced, the excitement mounting, "Let's settle for 110 for nine!"

"110 for nine it is," all chorused. But ten minutes passed and no wicket fell. With Cheetham shielding the tail, they might well hold out; his was the wicket we craved. Then, amid great excitement, Lock gave us our ninth victim — but it was not Cheetham. Time for one more over. "A wicket in the last over," I proposed, quite carried away; my new-found friends were unanimously in favour. This was exhilarating stuff. Not tense, where one sits hushed, heart in mouth, with the pain part of the enjoyment. No, this was sheer, heady elation. It was perhaps as well that this was the last over; I don't think we could have taken much more. Five balls were safely negotiated, and an air of sober reality began to assert itself; the crowd seemed to sense that the excitement was over for the day — that events had already exceeded their wildest dreams. "What a turn up if they were all out off the last ball," someone said. "Of course, the perfect ending!" we echoed. "A wicket off the last ball it shall be."

So much for wild optimism, however, when, with expectations of a fatal snick, a hoisted pull cleared the leg-trap and dropped half-way to the boundary. Lock was after it, and picked up just as the batsmen were completing their second run. "And again," they called, opting to take one for the throw, and to Lock of all people. That magnificent fielder turned and threw with unerring accuracy, and Heine, out by a margin, carried straight on to the pavilion. A wicket off the last ball. All out for 112. If we were all wrong with our forecasts, we were alright otherwise.

These companions had different seats for the next day, I never saw them again. But where else, other than at a cricket ground, could you establish such cordial rapport with passing strangers? Cricket, and especially good cricket, does things to people.

It was unlikely that Tuesday would produce quite the same thrills and, indeed, with England batting, who would have welcomed them? But cricket, like a woman, has many moods and aspects, and the next splendid day's play showed us more of them. The sun was up betimes, the day already hot when we arrived. One usually associates this with 500 runs and endless leather-chasing, but this was the Oval in the fifties. No more need be said.

260 runs in eight hours play hardly foretold a batsman's frolic, and in cold figures sounds dreadfully slow, yet here was tight rather than dull cricket. A turning pitch, top-class, spin-bowling and fielding ensured that runs had to be well earned. The prospect was of a day-long battle between Tayfield and the English batsmen. Lock (four for 39)

and Laker (two for 28) had accounted for six of South Africa's wickets, and though Tayfield (three for 39 in the first innings) had not the benefit of a comparable spinner at the other end, Goddard would make scoring difficult and they could count on excellent support in the field. On balance though, the precious 40 run lead secured on first innings, taken with the fact that South Africa would have to bat last, gave the advantage to England.

Hopes that England had, at least temporarily, found a new opening partnership were somewhat dashed when, almost before we had settled, Ikin edged Heine to slip — for nought. It looked as if May would again be cast as a virtual opener, but the rustic gait and sloping shoulders of the emerging figure did not belong to May. Ambling, instead, to the wicket was the genial figure of Tom Graveney, already with some, albeit unhappy, experience of opening, and sent in early to preserve May's wicket. Ironically, Graveney chose the most difficult pitch of the five on which to play his best innings of the series. It was not great numerically, nor by his highest standards, but, in context, it was a most timely effort. He and Close saw off the new ball, and took the score to 30 before Close was bowled by Goddard for 15. But these were only the pourparlers; the real test, the crucial dual that would possibly decide the match, was yet to come. Now, at 12.30, Tayfield came on to bowl.

May had since joined Graveney, well aware of the need for watchfulness in the critical hour before lunch. We had seen what Lock and Laker could do on this pitch; would Tayfield, who lost nothing by comparison, wreak similar destruction? Against less able batsmen, he might well have done, but May and Graveney saw to it that there would be no early collapse. At the same time they pushed on at a respectable rate. In fact, it would be hard to imagine either staying long at the crease without so doing. Both fluent stroke-players and fine timers of the ball, they took runs from easily-pushed placements when fours were hard to come by. Tayfield bowled few bad balls, and was seldom collared, but, like all great bowlers, he could be hit, as here by batsmen of true class, these two taking the score past ninety before the off-spinner bowled Graveney through the gate for 42. Graveney would play many bigger, yet less valuable, innings in the course of a long Test career. 95 for three. May 35 not out.

In largely holding Tayfield off, the honours of the morning belonged to England. Now, with a lead of 134 and May and Compton to take strike in the afternoon, they had to be in the driving seat.

The period between lunch and tea provided as fascinating a piece of cricket as one might hope to see. Needless to say, all the more strange then, it induced, at one stage, though only from a tiny minority, a slow hand-clap. "I don't know what more they want, this is tremendous cricket," said my neighbour. I didn't know either, and still don't.

No one, surely, came expecting the ball to be struck far and wide. More likely, the rattle of falling wickets. In fact, they got neither; but in the determined efforts of each side to achieve their ends, when at once every feature of good cricket was brought into play, those who had eyes to see witnessed an absorbing dual in the sun. For an hour, one had the spectacle of two superb stroke-players trying to wrest the initiative from a world class off-spinner bowling in helpful conditions and consistently to his field, a field moreover, that allowed nothing other than precise placement to get through. Ball after ball of Tayfield's described elevated curves, inviting the drive. Time and again, May and Compton with sweetly-struck strokes, forced him powerfully from the block-hole and away on the off-side, only to be thwarted by brilliant stops in the field. Even when they hit away from a fielder, an outstretched hand would suddenly appear. To see McGlew, like a goalkeeper, diving full-length in the covers, even though it prevented your own batsmen from scoring, was an unforgettable sight. Yet always there was a man backing up should one elude him. That, in seventy-five minutes, May and Compton, playing their shots, managed only sixty runs between them, says everything for the quality of the South African out-cricket. It was four or nothing it seemed, and usually nothing, yet when the batsmen did bisect the field, it was with strokes of high pedigree — as indeed they had to be. As my neighbour said . . .

Compton had made 30, when, having survived Tayfield, he was caught behind off Fuller. Like Graveney's, his innings could not be assessed numerically. That England were now 157 for four on a bowler's wicket — almost 200 runs on — gave a truer indication of its worth. If further testimony were needed, then the events of the next hour put the value of both Compton's and Graveney's contributions into even sharper focus.

May, now with 65 and again the bulwark of the England innings, could still look to Watson, Bailey, Spooner, and a useful tail, for the help he needed in building an unassailable lead. Another seventy or eighty would probably establish a task too great for South Africa. They, on the other hand, tenaciously as they had fought, were seeing the game slip away from them. They had played their trump card, and, well as Tayfield bowled, he had not wrought the havoc he might have done. Since half-past twelve he had wheeled away unchanged, yet had just the one wicket to show for it. Another top-class spinner would, no doubt, have made a difference, but, as it was, England had every reason to feel confident.

They had a few less, however, when, in little more time than it takes to tell, Watson 3, Bailey 1, and Spooner 0, had all come and gone, and England had slumped to 170 for seven. Tayfield had struck twice, and was at last, it seemed, reaping his reward. May, who had looked on helplessly from the other end, was 72 and in danger of being stranded. This is, in fact, what happened. Though Laker (12), and not for the first time, shaped better than some above him, Tayfield and Heine soon picked off the tail, leaving May high and dry on 89. If ever an innings rated a century, it was May's that day. England were all out for 204, the last six wickets having fallen for just 47 runs. Tayfield, operating unchanged from 12.30 to 6.30, finished with five for 60 from 53 overs — almost half the number bowled — in a wonderfully accurate, sustained spell of spin-bowling.

South Africa were left needing 243 to win — still no easy task, but an easier one than had seemed likely at tea. Someone, it is true, would have to play an outstanding innings, but could not the visitors provide such a one?

That is to talk dispassionately and with hindsight. Appraisal of a score or lead tends, one finds, to be influenced by your loyalties — whether your side is chasing or defending it; and usually the opposition seems the better placed! Thus, although on sober reflection, a target of 243 would always have taken some finding — and would we have fancied England to get it? — it did not, at the time, strike this cautious Briton as anything too demanding. And why, oh why, had England not made 300?

South Africa had the Wednesday and the Thursday in which to get the runs, yet time was really irrelevant. With the weather set fair, there was sure to be a result. Either they would make the runs with something to spare, or they would not make them at all. Batting through two whole days, even had they thought of doing so, was not to be contemplated. It was victory or nothing.

Next morning an expectant crowd watched Statham and Bailey begin their token stint prior to the entry of England's prospective match-winners, Lock and Laker. Goddard and McGlew saw them off safely enough, and soon their opening stand became a matter of concern to English hearts. They had made only twenty or so, but these were not known as punishing scorers. To see them batting so easily gave fears of what some of the others might do. However, thus far they had faced the sort of bowling to which openers are well accustomed. The real test was about to begin.

The appearance of Lock and Laker in the first innings had brought about a dramatic collapse; it was almost too much to hope that they, or Lock as it had been then, would meet with quite the instant success a second time. Yet, Lock was again soon in credit, having Goddard caught by Graveney for 20. 28 for one. Enter Keith, one of the disappointments of the series; how ironic if he should choose this match to excell. As one might expect from a number three, he was not without scoring strokes, and almost immediately unleashed a searing cover drive — a daisy cutter hit with the full face of the bat, and travelling like a bullet. One of three things might have occurred. It could have streaked past May at cover before he had time to move; it could have broken that fielder's ankle; it could have been half-stopped by an unwitting boot. In fact, none of these things happened. May, showing amazing reflexes, and to the astonishment of all concerned, stooped and picked the ball of his boot-laces, and a disbelieving Keith was out. A young man's catch, and what a moment to make it. 28 for two.

So Lock had struck again, but this time Laker was the quicker to respond. One run later he trapped Endean leg before wicket for 0, not long after that, disposed of McLean in similar fashion — and for a similar score. 33 for four, and the last three batsmen had made not a run between them. The arrival of Waite restored some sanity to the proceedings, and he and McGlew took the score to 59 before the irrepressible Lock at last got one past McGlew's bat. Cheetham now joined with Waite in the biggest stand so far, but at 88 the captain became another of Laker's leg before wicket victims. That, one thought, was surely that. But Waite, at least, was prepared to go down fighting.

He and Mansell added another thirty runs, in the process of which Waite reached a well-earned fifty; while he was there, South Africa still lived in hope. But the Surrey men were not to be denied. Lock now had Mansell caught for nine, and, without addition to the score, Laker claimed the vital wicket of Waite. His sixty was an admirable innings of no mean skill, and his dismissal a cruel blow to South Africa. 118 for eight. If only the others had done half as well.

As if, too, to show what might have been, Tayfield and Fuller put on 28, before a run-out fairly well typified South Africa's fortune that day. Laker finished the job by removing Heine at 151, and England had won by 92 runs.

It was a comfortable victory in the end, though to be charitable, South Africa could count themselves unfortunate on a number of counts. For one thing, they came up against Lock and Laker in conditions helpful to them, conditions they exploited to the full. Laker finished with figures of five for 56 from 37 overs, Lock four for 62 from 33, and between them they bowled 70 overs out of a total of 87. If proof were needed that bowlers hunt better in pairs, then here it was. Tayfield's wicket-run ratio was almost identical to Laker's, yet not until it was too late in the day did he made the same inroads into England's innings. A 'Lock' at the other end would, no doubt, have hastened matters.

Well as Lock and Laker bowled, though, Waite showed that they were not unplayable, and South Africa could not have envisaged the complete failure of three of their front-line batsmen. With modest contributions all down the line, Waite's innings might have been enough to see them home. Yet it is interesting to ponder how much May's catch influenced that early collapse. Perhaps not at all, but it is not unknown for single incidents to change the whole course of a match. Confidence is soon undermined, and the sight of a colleague caught off a scorching drive that barely left the ground, could have done nothing to persuade the South Africans that it was to be their day. No, without taking anything away from an England side whose all-round superiority deservedly saw them home, one has to say that from the start not too much went right for their opponents.

They lost the toss on a pitch the nature of which they can hardly have relished, and for which they were not the best equipped, while probably, on reflection, it was a mistake to leave out Winslow. South Africa's batting failed in both innings, and fifty from a hitter in a low-scoring match, apart from its intrinsic value, would have threatened the spinner's dominance. Maybe, too, it might have been wiser, if in some ways highly contentious, to have retained McGlew as captain, to the exclusion of the newly-fit Cheetham. Had McGlew not lead South Africa back into serious contention? But such is life. If things had been different, they would have been *totally* different.

After everything, England won an entertaining series three for two, and, taken overall, this was a fair result. At one time looking to carry all before them, they rather lost their way at Old Trafford and Leeds, creditably came back to take the last match fairly convincingly; or perhaps more accurately, did so in the end. Although South Africa were at no stage in the lead, and a 92 run defeat brooks little argument, neither could they have been considered out of it. England could never afford to feel complacent, and there was certainly no sense of anti-climax about the match. I am still of the opinion, that, on another day,

243, or at least something like it, was always possible. Clearly, they could bat a good deal better, and, as it was, not too much more was needed to have given them a chance. After a sound start it required only one aggressive innings to have put the pressure on England. And, as it pleases me to think, but for May's timely catch, who knows?

And that really is the story of 1955 — a fine, close-fought rubber, played in admirable spirit, and blessed with wonderful weather. Little of note took place outside it. Surrey claimed their fourth successive championship with an air of inevitability that suggested that it would be neither easily or quickly wrested from them. With Laker, Lock and Loader yet to reach their peak, and Bedser still a very good county bowler, plus skipper Surridge and Eric Bedser, they were ensured the best attack in the land for many years to come. It was often said that the batting was weak, but surely this was true only comparatively. Weak, with players like May, Barrington, Constable and Tom Clark in the order? They may have lacked solidity all through, but somebody invariably came off. At any rate, they made enough runs for their bowlers to obtain results — the proof of the pudding.

Otherwise, though, the county programme was for the most part unexceptional. This was not a season of super statistics, or of mammoth scores and records tumbling by the day. It was not a year that writers enthuse over though, perhaps surprisingly. The year 1955 saw one of the most enjoyable Test series since the war, full of fine batting and bowling and, need one say, superb fielding. But, more than that, it was a season of light and laughter, cordiality and day-long sunshine — of an atmosphere, and a pleasant one at that. Jack Cheetham's South Africans will be remembered if only because they brought so perfect a summer.

VIII – End of an Era

My last choice is rather a personal one, and perhaps owes its inclusion as much to sentiment as to the quality of its cricket. This is to say, I can never be sure whether I felt the same way about it then, as I do now. Probably not, yet that scarcely matters — if a season evokes fond memories, then it must, for whatever reason, be worthy of recall. The year 1938 may not, cricket-wise, have been a vintage year, though much, of course, has been written about it, but I feel I am not alone in thinking that it conjures a nostalgia all its own, and I wonder how many contemporaries will know just what I mean.

This was not the finest summer of the thirties, though by no means a poor one, and August certainly lived up to expectations. Nevertheless, conditions hardly made it a fair contest of bat and ball — as, say, O'Reilly and Fleetwood-Smith would have testified — and bowlers toiled mostly at disadvantage. But, on the credit side, the Australians were here, at least three historic innings were played, and there were enough records, incidents and rare occurrences to keep most people happy. Yet, more than that, and why I suspect that the passage of time may well have enhanced its memory, 1938 was to be the last pukka season before the lights went out in Europe. In short, as no one could have foreseen, this was the end of an era — not just for cricket, but for a whole way of life; for, had one but known, things would never be quite the same again.

Sentimental burblings of one whose best years are behind him? A sighing for the empire of one living out his present in the days of the past? Not quite. I venture to state that anyone whose life fairly spanned the war years will — subconsciously at least — view those periods as two separate entities, with no bridge between, as if a full-stop had been drawn across the face of time. One suddenly finds oneself six years older, yet fondly imagining one can slip back to so-called 'normality'. But, whatever else wars bring in their wake, they certainly bring change — though not always for the better — and change, from the familiar to the unfamiliar, is seldom to our liking. Inevitably, a part of us gets left behind. Try as one may, one can never quite pick up the old threads. Of course, life goes on; there were, as always, good days ahead — 1947 for instance — but, for better or worse, we had said goodbye to an established way of life we had thought was with us for all time.

There was much that was bad in the thirties, in a world that is often bad, but 1938 was a time of great economic recovery, of stable prices and cheap goods. If one worked, life was comfortable, and, whether my fancy or not, seemed to convey a far greater sense of serenity than exists at the present time. We must not get carried away, however; this is not a book about social conditions through the ages. This is a book about memorable cricket seasons, and the point here, is that, in keeping with the era, cricket too, reflected the established order — sacrosanct, four-square, not given to radical change. Also, with fewer distractions, we attached more prominence to its annual arrival. Newspapers, not preoccupied with nuclear arms and industrial disputes, saw Test Matches as front page news. Bradman, Hammond and Hutton were the big names of the day; what is more, we had it on good authority, that there would be 'Peace in Our Time'. That was something to know. Now we could settle down and return to more pressing matters — the biennial fight for the Ashes. Let us hark back then, to the great run feast of 1938.

There was something about an Australian visit in those days, that is not quite so apparent today. The reasons for this are, I think, fairly clear. With less Test cricket generally, and little or no coverage of tours abroad, these were virtually for most of us, four-year encounters. Then again, Australia were at that time the only country to fully arouse public interest. True, the last South African side of 1935 had managed to win the one match that was finished, and so clinched the rubber, but they were not yet regarded as a major draw. It was the men in the baggy green caps who really caught the imagination; the more so when they numbered among them the 'Boy from Bowral', Donald George Bradman.

Love him or hate him — and memories of his previous two visits gave just cause for the latter — one had to concede that, in Bradman, we were privileged to watch one of the very few players who can rightly be termed 'great', someone who, on good wickets, was arguably the greatest batsman of all time. True, I cannot honestly say I regarded his merciless hammering of England's attack for 974 runs in 1930 with undue ecstacy, but here, a little older if not wiser, I could more appreciate the man for what he was — an awesome opponent, a run machine without precedent, and, of course, a tremendous crowd-puller.

Appointed to the captaincy for the 1936–37 series, Bradman had responded by leading Australia back from two-down to defeat Gubby Allen's side three for two, and was now here, as captain, for the first time. He showed in leadership the same uncompromising approach that he brought to his batting — clinical, you might say ruthless. This, allied to a shrewd cricketing brain, ranks him among the best of international captains, and, without doubt, had much to do with Australia's run of near unbroken success during his reign. It might be argued that Bradman always had charge of strong sides. But this would not be quite true. Certainly, those he led in post-war years did not require too much motivating, but the mid-thirties had marked the end of an era in Australian cricket, when many of the familiar older players — Woodfull, Ponsford, Oldfield, Grimmett — all departed together. This, together with the tragic death of Archie Jackson, aged twenty-four, the most gifted young opener seen for many years, meant that Bradman took over the leadership during a time of transition. It is more than possible that his captaincy had tipped the balance in 1936–37 (did he not once tell his bowlers not to take wickets until the pitch had dried out?), and the team he brought here in 1938 could not be called one of Australia's best.

All things are relative, however; it was patently not a weak side — Bradman's presence alone ensured that — but it was woefully short of fast bowling, and wanted for an established opening pair, a plight worsened by a shipboard injury to Sid Barnes, who did not regain fitness until the final Test. Eleven of the party were unused to English conditions, only five players — McCabe, Brown, Chipperfield, O'Reilly and Bradman himself — remaining of the 1934 side. Clearly much depended on their form and, as with any touring side, on how many of the newcomers came good.

All this gave food for speculation as the spring of 1938 found us eagerly anticipating both the arrival of the traditional foe, and the prospects of the home side. With a poor regard for hospitality, one hoped, somewhat paradoxically, to send those long-awaited visitors back a good deal less pleased with life than when they came. Many of the English players lined up to do battle here will not be new to us — Compton, for example, appears for a third time — but on the premise that you cannot have too much of a good thing, let us embark upon another season of their exploits.

By chance, I have before me a set of cigarette cards comprising the leading cricketers of that year — a relic from those happy days when small boys waylaid owners of newly-acquired packs with cries of: "Let's have your fag card please mister," and, more often than not, came away clutching a prize. This particular set, however, entered my possession by the more simple expedient of persuading a gullible nephew to part with a complete series in exchange for an unnamed sum. Well-worn now, after forty years of sorting out 'best elevens', the subjects of this rare collector's item remain as fresh, and as young, to my mind today, as they did then. Portrayed are thirty-four Englishmen from Ames to Yardley, plus the Australian touring party.

Ames for one needs no introduction, receiving more than a mention in our review of 1928. Still the best wicket-keeper in England, and a batsman good enough to make the Hundred Century Club, only injury kept him out of two of the Tests here. Number two, Charlie Barnett, opened the innings with Hutton, and was a remarkably quick scorer for one of that breed. Skipping a few now, we come to a youthful-looking Bill Edrich, who, alas, proved one of the failures of this series. A young player of immense potential, he made his point early on by scoring 1,000 runs before the end of May, every one of those runs coming at Lords, incidentally. Such a broad hint could hardly be ignored, and Edrich was given every chance to make good, yet in a year of plumb wickets, and big totals, with runs there for the taking, he never once threatened to repeat that sort of form. Serious doubts arose as to his big-match temperament, and some muttered that he was fortunate, at this time, to be given so extended a run. Yet Edrich was persevered with on the tour of South Africa that winter and, when at last he did come good, did so in style with a typically aggressive 219. Later, in a bigger 'Test', he displayed enough temperament to win the D.F.C. with the R.A.F. and, as we know, was to play his best cricket for England in the post-war years. The year 1938, for him, was just one of cricket's enigmas.

After 'E' comes 'F', which brings us to another England regular, Kenneth Farnes, the only fast bowler to appear in every Test, though there were only four played — the Manchester match being abandoned without a ball bowled. England were hit by a curious injury jinx this summer, and Farnes was one of the few ever-presents. It was just as well he was too, for although there was no shortage of quick bowlers around the counties, only those of genuine pace could hope to get the ball past the bat on the type of Test wickets encountered here. Anything less against men like Bradman and McCabe was little more than a burnt offering. Farnes had that extra yard of pace with which to extract life, as too, had Bowes, who played in two of the Tests, but, in the absence of Voce, another who could hurry them through, it was significant that England looked to the medium-paced leg-breaks of Doug Wright to bear the brunt of the bowling, in much the same way as Australia used O'Reilly. Farnes it was, though, like many an Essex paceman before and since, who spearheaded the attack, and it is sad to think that only three years later, a brave Pilot Officer made the ultimate sacrifice for his country.

Moving on, the next names among my gallery that rivet attention follow in quick succession. And what names — Hammond, Hardstaff and Hutton, three who were to make a tidy number of runs before the series was out. Walter Hammond, for long England's premier batsman, had recently acquired amateur status, and in so doing had become the natural successor to the captaincy. It was some measure of his standing among cricketers, that no one, by word or deed, sought to query this appointment — any more than it occurred to call for his head during his abysmal run of low scores in 1934. One would sooner have censored the Archbishop of Canterbury. Hammond was above criticism, his supremacy unquestioned. That he was neither the best nor the most enterprising of captains did not come in to it; once Hammond W. R. became W. R. Hammond, it was automatically assumed that 'Wally' would lead them out.

In fairness, it was this very mantle of greatness, rather than tactical inadequacies, that tended to make Hammond an undistinguished leader. It set him apart from his fellows. Supremely confident himself, though devoid of arrogance, he failed to appreciate that others less gifted might be in need of encouragement. The thought never occurred to him; he took his talents for granted, and simply could not understand that players and public alike looked up to him. Though held in awe by others, Hammond saw nothing to greatly esteem in himself. This failure to appreciate his own powers resulted in a signal failure to inspire. It was not errors in the field that drew subsequent criticism of Hammond's leadership — he made few — but the appearance he gave of being content merely to stand by and let the game drift on. His authority derived from his immense playing skills, rather than from any sense of personal magnetism. Hammond's inability to communicate has brought charges of aloofness, charges which one thinks unjustified. He had a certain reserve that gave him an air of detachment; he was also a man of moods, but he was not aloof in the sense that Jardine was aloof — that is to say, he was not aware of it. Hammond was simply Hammond; he neither sought popularity, nor invited enmity. He made no attempt to 'sell himself' with a false bonhommie contrary to his nature; he just did the right things that were expected of his office, and assumed that people understood his actions, because they seemed natural enough to him. For twenty years England's leading cricketer, Walter Hammond, in the end, was a victim of his own greatness.

So here offered the rare prospect of the champions of each country leading their sides into combat. Hammond and Bradman in direct opposition — each only too conscious that the other stood potentially as the chief source of his team's runs, and constituted as such the wicket most to be striven for. If Bradman showed himself to be the more positive captain, Hammond, it seemed, had a wider range of strength at his disposal, always allowing, of course, that England could field her strongest side — which, in the event, she was far from able to do. Not that the reserves were in any way inadequate; this was an era of great prosperity, at least for batsmen. But here, demands went beyond that of the odd replacement, and, at Leeds, for example, they were sending round for players on the day of the match. However, we were not to know this, and, prior to the first Test, could rest content that any number of permutations could produce a side that looked good enough to make a serious bid for those, by now rather mystical, yet nevertheless, much coveted, Ashes. But we have yet to complete a review of the troops called to the colours.

Hutton and Hardstaff have been discussed at length elsewhere, and, in any case, Hutton was not exactly anonymous this summer, and is due for a 'good innings' later on. Compton's pedigree too, we can take as read. That leaves one batting place not spoken for — and who was recalled after two series in the wilderness? Why, that true Lancashire lad, the hero of Brisbane in 1932–3, Eddie Paynter. After his success with Jardine's 'bodyline' side, it seems incredible that he should have been passed over for the next two Australian campaigns — the more so in the light of England having lost them both, the first, in 1934, rather badly. Now reinstated, he was again to show his mettle, doing well both here and on the subsequent tour of South Africa. So it was not only the selectors of 1902 who had blind spots; to err is human and ever will be.

The choice of Paynter thus completed what was, by any criteria, a formidable batting line-up. Seven batsmen, if you counted Ames — and you had to count Ames — left room for only four bowlers. However, the presence of Edrich, Hammond and Compton, if necessary, lent weight to the attack, and so permitted the luxury of an extra batsman. The only regular bowler not yet mentioned was Verity, another in a long line of Great Yorkshire left-arm spinners, and as sure of his place at this time as was Rhodes thirty years before. First capped against New Zealand in 1931, he had been an almost permanent fixture of the England side ever since. With two Australian tours and a return series behind him, Verity knew all about Bradman — more importantly, how to get him out, having done so twice in the Lord's match of 1934. However, that was on a helpful pitch where he took fifteen wickets for 104. Given normal conditions, bowling to 'The Don' was likely to prove an unprofitable experience and Verity, no less than anyone else, was well aware that a good many hours of fruitless toil lay in store. On plumb wickets, the chief recourse for bowlers of his type lay in accuracy, variation of flight — and infinite patience. Two hundred wickets in each of the previous three seasons suggested he had those qualities in abundance.

Furthermore, Verity's ability to defend stoutly with the bat meant that the 'tail' commenced at nine. I say 'defend', because he was not a great stroke-maker, though neither was he purely obstructive, and with sound, rather than fluent, batting he had made his forties in Tests. Twice in his career, Verity took ten wickets in an innings — once for ten runs — and, against Essex in 1933, returned match figures of seventeen for 91. But he, alas, was another who, unbeknown, was playing for the last time against Australia. Five years later, a man who, as a cricketer had served England nobly, gave his life in a larger cause, killed in action during the North African campaign. The text on his cigarette card informs us that Hedley Verity was born in 1905; it could not predict that Captain Verity was to die with honours in 1943. The future is not our's to see.

Nevertheless, one did not need to be a clairvoyant to forecast that it was not the bowlers who were to make the news this summer — at least, not in the way they sought! Short of a downpour, these wickets would show no mercy — Trent Bridge, its old feather-bed self; the Oval as responsive as a wet doormat. Here, containment was the order of the day, wickets a welcome bonus. Whether quickly, or in the batsman's own time, the runs would surely come — as early portents clearly indicated.

With the season only a few weeks old, Edrich, as we say, had already notched up a 1,000 runs at Headquarters, which, apart from its worth as a cricketing curio, rather implied that the Lord's track was not in too bad a shape either. And Edrich, be it remembered, was a new boy; what might Hammond, Hutton and the rest achieve in these conditions? We all know, of course, something of what 'Hammond and the rest' achieved, but, to capture the mood of the day, let us pretend that it is all to come, as we awaited the announcement of the teams for the Nottingham Test.

Here, at least, though you might juggle with a place or two, was about the best team that England could call upon, and, without question, one of the strongest batting sides ever to take the field. What bowler would not shudder at the sight of this line-up; Hutton, Barnett, Edrich, Hammond, Paynter, Compton, Ames, Verity, Sinfield (his only Test), Farnes and Wright? Was it unreasonable to suppose that Australia would be hard put to bowl them out twice? — or even once! The bowling suffered only by comparison. Taken on its own, England would have been very glad of this attack in the immediate post-war years, it being well-balanced, if perhaps wanting for another bowler of genuine pace. It certainly appeared to be stronger and better-balanced than that of the Australians, who leaned heavily on the medium-paced wrist spin of O'Reilly and the slow left-arm of L.O'B. Fleetwood-Smith, both, admittedly, experienced Test Bowlers. Apart from the decidedly quick, but erratic, McCormick, and McCabe the auxiliary seamer, the rest were all pretty much untried, and had done nothing in the early matches to suggest that they would post any problems here. The batting looked solid enough down to number five, with Bradman, Hasset and McCabe to follow openers Brown and Fingleton, but thereafter carried nothing like the weight of England's middle order. However, when it came to comparing strengths, there was one factor that could never be sufficiently allowed for — D. G. Bradman.

It is said that the mark of a truly great player is revealed when his dominance forces changes in the way the game is played. Just as Grace nullified pure fast-bowling, and Hammond's off-side play obliged opponents to attack his leg stump, so Bradman's capacity for large, often very large, scores brought about a whole new conception of what constituted a good innings total. Prior to 1930, 400 was considered 'safe', as indeed it would be today. The advent of Bradman changed all that. In that year, at Lords, England's first innings score of 425 — of which Duleepsinji made 173 before throwing his wicket away — proved not nearly enough, resulting in defeat by seven wickets. From then on, opposing captains had to think differently. If Bradman could make his double, and even treble centuries at will, totals would have to be judged accordingly; now, sides could hardly feel secure if an innings failed to reach at least 500.

Nor, so far on this tour, had Bradman shown any signs that his powers were diminishing. Three times he had visited England, and three times he had begun with a double century in the opening match at

Worcester. Like Edrich, Bradman too had made 1,000 runs before the end of May, just as he had done in 1930, and he arrived at the first Test with a batting average of over 150. It was with something like relieved pleasure that you got him out for 'just' 100! On his favourite ground, Leeds, Bradman did not consider that he had had a proper innings until he had made three times that number — all in the one day, of course. How could you legislate for such a man?

★ ★ ★ ★ ★ ★

Trent Bridge, Nottingham. As always, an exceedingly good toss to win. Whatever Hammond's failings as a captain, losing these was not one of them. Four wins out of four was his record in this series, and here he had no hesitation in opting to take first innings. (W. G. used to say, "Always consider putting the other side in — then bat," but one doubts if Hammond deliberated long at Trent Bridge.) Hutton and Barnett, particularly the latter, now demonstrated just why batsmen hankered so much to bat there. Hutton, by nature the more sedate player, was also, at twenty-two, making his first appearance against Australia, and, understandably, on a wicket full of runs, was content to go quietly along at his accustomed pace. Barnett, on the other hand, was not new to the Test scene, and in any case, was committed to an attacking game. He displayed a full range of strokes right from the start and, in the event, failed by just one run to reach a hundred before lunch. Nevertheless, in the afternoon, both men, Barnett 126, and Hutton exactly 100, went on to complete fine centuries.

This was an excellent start, and, although neither Edrich nor Hammond added to Australia's misery, Paynter and Compton now came together in a stand of 206, an English record for the fifth wicket. Compton, like Hutton, was playing against Australia for the first time, and he too attained the distinction of making a century — a distinction, however, that did not earn his captain's unstinted praise. Shortly after reaching his hundred, Compton played a careless stroke to be out for 102, and Hammond was not at all pleased at this needless sacrifice of a wicket. He was, of course, correct to try to harness the ability of a young player to the needs of the side, but, with England close to 500, five wickets in hand, and Paynter well entrenched, would Hammond have acted thus but for the insecurity induced by the threat of Bradman?

Any last worries the England captain might have harboured were put to rest as the gritty Poynter took his score past two hundred, putting

England in an unassailable position at 658 for eight. Hammond at last felt that he had enough runs on the board, and at this point declared the innings closed, with Paynter 216 not out. Well into the second day, Australia, with nothing but a draw to play for, set out on their long haul. At 194 for six, of which Brown had made 48 and Bradman 51, they were in trouble. But at this point, with the follow-on beckoning, and an innings defeat more than a possibility, McCabe proceeded to play one of the great Test match innings.

Shielding each partner in turn, he farmed the bowling to such an extent that, in barely four hours, he made 232 out of the 300 scored while he was at the wicket. The longer he batted, the faster he went, and, of the 77 added for the last wicket, McCabe's share was 72. With a power born of perfect timing, he played all the strokes equally well, but his fierce hooking, often off his eyebrows, presented a particularly thrilling spectacle. When the ball was pitched up, he drove forcefully through the covers or back over the bowler's head; anything short was thumped away square on either side of the wicket, his cutting and pulling being scarcely less savage than his hooking. It was this innings that prompted Bradman to call his players to the dressing room window, with: "Come and look at this; you may never see its like again." And later, when McCabe came in, he was greeted with: "I'd have given a good deal to have played an innings like that one." Praise from 'The Don' was praise indeed.

Despite McCabe's heroics, Australia's reply of 411 was still not enough to avert the follow-on; there was some batting to be done yet if they were to save the match and go to Lords all-square. Bill Brown, in the continued absence of new hope Barnes, was far away and Australia's most reliable opener on this tour, and now knuckled down to his accustomed role of sheet-anchor. Soon joined by Bradman, these two, bent only on survival, ground their way to match-saving centuries. Brown, who stayed five-and-a-half hours, was eventually out for 133, but, by then, Australia were in front and the game saved. Bradman batted even longer, playing one of the best defensive innings of his career, ending with 144 not out. That Australia, at 427 for six, led by 180 runs was purely of academic interest. Only England had ever looked like winning, and England had been denied.

The only victor was the pitch, even that notoriously placid strip surpassing itself; in all 1,500 runs were scored, including five single, and two double centuries, while only twenty-four wickets fell. Was this the shape of things to come, we asked? With these batting sides, and on these pitches, was a result ever likely? Verity, the best finger-spinner of the day, bowled 62 overs in Australia's second innings with scant success. O'Reilly, the most purely attacking bowler on either side, had toiled away for figures of three for 164. As the 'Tiger' drily observed, "He and Fleetwood-Smith (four for 153) hadn't been loafing".

It was not, of course, that the cricket was boring or lacked purpose. There was nothing dreary about the batting of Barnett and Compton, and I'll wager that no one nodded off during McCabe's onslaught. There was no want of technical merit either in the innings of Hutton, Paynter, Brown and Bradman. No, concern here was that if a score of 650 did not ensure victory, then how could England ever hope to regain the Ashes? There was a feeling too, that, without detracting from McCabe's heroic effort, Australia had been allowed back into the game, and that so good an opportunity might not again present itself. The match was all but won, thought the man in the street. But, as we know, counting chickens in a game with the vagaries of cricket, is not to be recommended.

So on to Lords, the cricketing Mecca for visiting sides, the ground where all players especially hope to do well. Success is welcome anywhere, yet it is fair to say that to make a hundred or to take five wickets at Headquarters is the secret ambition of every cricketer. For the public also, the Lord's Test is a major occasion on the sporting calendar — an event to rank with Henley, Wimbledon or Royal Ascot. Here, traditionally, the reigning Monarch graces the Monday with their presence, the teams being presented in the afternoon. To my mind, the atmosphere of Lords is unique; less partisan than Headingley or Old Trafford; more lovely than the Oval, and blessed with a slightly more sporting wicket than Trent Bridge. At least it was so in pre-war days, when none were more keen to leave their mark on the hallowed turf than those from the far-flung Commonwealth.

Thus in every sense, the Lord's match was a little special. Set in the heart of the Metropolis, it served as the show-piece of the series, the players more conscious here, perhaps, of the spotlight's glare, of the eyes of the world or, at least, the nation being upon them. If personal triumph was doubly sweet, then failure was twice confounded. Like fluffing one's lines at the Old Vic. The pitch, true and firm, as all wickets should be, was yet fast enough to allow for good cricket. Here, in the fine weather of 1930, Australia had made a record 729, to win by seven wickets; in the damp conditions of 1934, they were put to rout in 'Verity's Match'. What, one wondered, had 1938 in store?

England made only one change for this match, Wellard, the Somerset fast bowler and renowned big-hitter, coming in for Sinfield, who in any case had not been a first choice at Nottingham. Allowing that, at no time, were all the best players available together, this was probably as good a side, if not better, than any of the other three put out that year. For Australia, Chipperfield, a batsman-cum-spin bowler replaced Ward, a bowler, but, in truth, juggle as they might, nothing could disguise the fact that they were a three-man bowling side. Not *quite* perhaps, since O'Reilly, in some senses, was at least two bowlers — first, in that he was both spinner and stock-bowler; second, that a fiercely competitive spirit urged him to all-out aggression, and a need to bowl his heart out. They did not call him Tiger for nothing. It was a pity, from Australia's point of view, that he could not go on at both ends. O'Reilly, one imagines, would have approved highly of that arrangement.

The preliminaries were soon over. Hammond again observed the first duty of a captain, and, again, could not have wavered long over his decision to bat. This time, though, he did not get the start he would have liked, Hutton, Barnett and the luckless Edrich, all falling to McCormick, in a lively opening spell, for just 31 runs. It's an ill-wind, however; one fancies that their speedy departure worked to the ultimate good of England — and cricket. The best innings are usually inspired by adversity and played when most needed. That situation was surely at hand. Hammond, as skipper, now had a chance to do what he did best — lead by example. England was sorely in need of a captain's innings; England was not disappointed.

There have been faster, perhaps more exciting, innings, innings where the ball was struck higher and further, and where the heart beat more rapidly, but for sheer majesty, grace and effortless power, this pastoral of Hammond's can rarely have been surpassed. Supported by Paynter, he at first played watchfully yet unhurriedly, stroking his ones and twos whither he chose. Then, the crisis passed, Hammond, as only he could, sought to impose his authority with those superb drives through the covers. His stroke-play blossomed. Time and again the ball cannoned back off the boundary rails, as now, totally in command, Hammond displayed the full extent of his repertoire. The straight drive, hammered back past the bowler; the easy pull to mid-wicket; the cut, the glance, the sweep — all were there — but mostly it was the lordly splendour of his off-side strokes, played with the full flow of the bat, that had a breathless crowd wreathed in ecstasy. How privileged they were. Hammond's hundred came with a sureness one took for granted, as did a second before the day was out; yet runs were almost incidental when you were lost in rapture of supreme batsmanship —

batsmanship that was pure art, with no hint of force, no trace of desperation.

Was there a finer sight in all England than Hammond in June sunshine, monarch of all he surveyed, parading the talents with which he was so richly endowed? Shirt sleeves buttoned at the wrist; blue silk handkerchief peeping from the pocket — trademarks of a nation's idol. Standing in splendid isolation, immaculate in every sense, impassive, betraying no emotion. Each movement that of a born athlete; each eloquent stroke belying a latent, rippling power. Lord Hammond indeed. Two hundred and ten not out at the close, he came in to an ovation that lingers yet, and was accorded an honour reserved only for the most moving occasions. The members rose to him, the applause echoing long after his majestic figure had disappeared from view.

A chanceless innings? Not quite. Late in the day, Chipperfield got half a hand to a skimming straight drive that succeeded in breaking the fielder's finger before continuing, and then rebounding yards from the pavilion fence. No one, shall we say, accused Chipperfield of dropping a catch.

And what of Paynter all this while? The game Lancastrian did well enough on his own account, unluckily being dismissed when just one short of his hundred. But, however brave his contribution, this day belonged to one man only, as did the next morning, when Hammond, resuming in much the same vein, added another 30 no less elegant runs. His 240 contained in all 32 boundaries, and with Ames going on to make 83, England were eventually all out for 494.

Nothing now was likely to impress more than Hammond's historic innings, but, in a very different way, Australia had their own hero when their turn came to bat. Bill Brown, whose patient innings had done so much to save the game at Nottingham, again dropped anchor as wickets fell steadily, if not rapidly, at the other end. Hasset made 56, McCabe 38 and O'Reilly a fighting 42 that he did not forget in a hurry, but no one really threatened to play a big innings. No one, that is, except Brown.

A neat, unobtrusive player, the quiet Queenslander, who had made a hundred here four years before, grafted steadily while his partners came and went. Brown, in fact, saw Australia through a mini-crisis, when, at 276 for four, Badcock 0, Ben Barnett 8, and Chipperfield 1, all fell in quick succession. It was here that O'Reilly showed us that he was more than just Australia's best bowler, first stopping the rot, then staying with Brown to see them to 400. That was the last stand of any consequence, and Brown soon ran out of partners after reaching an undefeated 202 out of a total of 422. It was a fine innings, full of character, and calling for great powers of concentration — and no less valuable to his side than was Hammond's for England. Australia trailed by 72 on first innings.

England failed to capitalise upon their lead, however, the early batting again falling to the pace of McCormick. In fact, there was a time on the fourth day when they looked to be in some danger, only for Compton, showing remarkable maturity for a young man of 20, to come to the rescue with a typical saving innings of 76 not out, which enabled Hammond to set Australia 314 to win in roughly four hours. Compton, so often to be a saviour of lost causes, showed here that, like his great contemporary Hutton, he was here to stay.

Despite an unbeaten century by Bradman (102), Australia never looked like reaching what was in any case an unlikely target, finishing at 204 for the loss of six wickets. This left England having had the better of two drawn games — one overwhelmingly so — but with nothing tangible to show for it. The last match, at the Oval, was to be played to a finish, where, in theory, England's longer batting was likely to hold the key, though there was always the sobering thought that Bradman was capable of running up a respectable innings total on his own. Naturally, much would depend on the state of the series when they arrived there, and the general opinion was that Hammond would be quite happy to go into the last match all-square. This was probably based on the reasoning that England had so far had the better of the luck without turning it to advantage; these things usually evened themselves out, and, that being the case, they might be glad to escape with a draw if, say, caught on a bad wicket at either Manchester or Leeds (we were not then to know that the Old Trafford game would be washed out). Their best chance, therefore, appeared to be at the Oval, where, on an assured batting pitch, a repeat of their Nottingham performance would surely give England victory. Many factors came into it, of course, not least the toss, and all this was, anyway, pure supposition. Hammond himself might well have had different thoughts. Much could happen before then.

As we say, the game at Manchester never started and, at first hand, I cannot recall another instance where not a ball was bowled.* So on to Leeds, not a happy venue for England over the years, particularly in the 'thirties. Memories of Bradman's two triple centuries there, in 1930 and 1934, the first a Test Match record, were still fresh in the mind.

*Old Trafford, 1890
Melbourne, Third Test, 1970–1.

Though he had managed two centuries in this series, he had yet to produce a really big one. Perhaps he was saving this for his favourite ground.

True to form, things started to go wrong for England even before the match began. Hutton broke a finger, Ames hurt his back, while a natural replacement, Leyland — unaccountably passed over thus far — ended all possible conjecture by breaking a thumb. Just why Maurice Leyland had been overlooked was again something known only to the selectors. A huge success on the 1936–37 tour, and one of the most consistent scorers in Test match history, he had time and again shown himself England's saviour during his ten years in Test cricket. Seven centuries against Australia speaks highly enough, but does not tell how often these were made in time of crisis, nor that many of his smaller contributions were every bit as valuable. Leyland was not the type of player who capitalised on solid starts; rather, he was at his best after the fall of early wickets and then, his side seen to safety, would be content. His hundred made, he rarely went on to 150. More effective than stylish, this plucky Yorkshire left-hander also bowled the 'chinaman' to good purpose, and was a player that any captain would want in his side. Of terse wit, Leyland's most oft-quoted remark typifies his fighting spirit. Asked, during the storm of 1932–33, how he viewed 'bodyline', he replied: "None of us likes it, but we don't all let on about it."

Still only thirty-eight, it could not have been his age that was against him, and we shall never be any the wiser as to why he was not brought in until the final Test. There was, of course, the matter of whom to leave out — you couldn't call it a problem since Edrich was the obvious candidate; yet it could be said that young players had to be brought on and given a fair trial, which perhaps points us some of the way to an explanation. However, Leyland's injury settled all argument here and, in the event, Edrich moved up to partner Barnett, allowing Hardstaff to come in lower down, while Fred Price of Middlesex took over the gloves from Ames. The other change was simply that of replacing one pace-bowler with another, Bowes being preferred to Wellard, but, whichever way you looked at it England, without Ames, were a batsman short without gaining the compensation of an extra bowler. A wicket-keeper who can bat well is indeed a priceless asset.

For Australia, Waite, a swing-bowler cum batsman, was brought in to supplement an overworked attack, Hammond having effectively removed Chipperfield from the firing-line. This was the only change in a side of which nine players appeared in every Test. Again though, this was largely a case of Hobson's choice. While Sid Barnes fretted all summer at his enforced absence, none of the other new players in the party seemed ripe for selection, and the Australian Board, too, had had some explaining to do for neglecting to bring Clarrie Grimmett, Australia's top wicket-taker at that time. Admittedly, he was now forty-five, yet, according to his friend and bowling partner, O'Reilly, 'Scarl' would not only have taken wickets on this tour, but also in another, had there been one. Another wrist-spinner of class could only have strengthened the attack, and, at the same time, reduced the burden on O'Reilly and Fleetwood-Smith. But this is hindsight again. As things were, a lightweight attack was obliged to cope as best it may, which, taken by and large, it did not do at all badly.

Headingley, at any rate, offered hope for the bowlers. If the wicket itself was not over-responsive, a combination of Pennine mist and murky light made batting as unpleasant a prospect as it had been so far, and, psychologically at least, the advantage lay with the ball. O'Reilly himself said that the pitch took no appreciable amount of spin, but once that doubt existed in the batsmen's minds they could no longer attack him with confidence. Thus, bowlers could set attacking fields and bowl accordingly. Runs had to be worked for, and a low-scoring match ensued.

In fact, in terms of ebb and flow, this was easily the best of the four games — further evidence that an even balance between bat and ball makes for more interesting cricket. Hammond again won the toss, but thereafter his captaincy left something to be desired, and there were some signs here that he was playing for the Oval. But then, I suppose that all the best captains are in the pavilion, and most of them have got whiskers.

England made heavy weather of it on the first day, when O'Reilly (five for 66) and Fleetwood-Smith (three for 73) were largely responsible for their being bowled out an hour before the close for 223, of which Hammond made 76. O'Reilly, at last getting some encouragement — not that he needed much — showed all his attacking propensities by clean bowling Edrich, Hammond and Compton — no mean feat against top batsmen not looking to attack. He had begun the series needing 20 wickets to make it 100 against England; three at Trent Bridge, six at Lords, and now five here put him within six of his target. On this form who could deny him?

In reply, Australia had fifty minutes to negotiate, during which time Wright took the wicket of Brown (for 22), wicket-keeper Barnett coming in as nightwatchman. They resumed next morning, at 32 for one, in heavy mist, the light growing steadily worse. No doubt an appeal would have been upheld, but Bradman, in a position for the first time to force a victory, wanted all the hours at his disposal. Nevertheless, the English swing-bowlers must have fancied their chances in these conditions, where Bowes with his movement off the seam, was particularly at home.

Fingleton was the first to go, out for 30, the score now 87 for two. This brought in Bradman, who had never found difficulty batting in bad light. If the ever-worsening gloom bothered him here, he showed little sign of it. Against the swing, pace and lift of Farnes and Bowes, he needed to summon every ounce of concentration, yet, despite a diffident beginning — Bradman was often a shaky starter — he made 103 in 165 minutes, a remarkable innings in the circumstances. No early breakthrough was forthcoming at the other end either, nightwatchman Barnett going beyond the call of duty in holding England up with a brave and invaluable innings of 57. The rest contributed almost nothing, but, thanks to these two, Australia secured a lead of 19 on the first innings, being all our for 242 at 5.15 on the second day.

But why, oh why, did Wright bowl only 15 overs — 15 overs from which he took two for 38, and those the wickets of Brown and Hasset? Of similar type to O'Reilly,* without perhaps having quite the Australian's control, Wright nevertheless posed problems for most batsmen, and might well have induced an error from Bradman, who had generally looked fairly comfortable against the quick men. He could be expensive, of course, and England were not defending too large a total, but, as is one of the penalties of leadership, Hammond came in for a good deal of criticism for what was widely viewed as an ultra-defensive policy. Was he playing for the Oval — or was this an early sign of Hammond's tendency to let the game drift?

The answer might be deduced from the fact that although the light was thought to have improved at the start of England's second innings, Barnett and Edrich immediately lodged an appeal, which was upheld. Ten minutes later, though, it was deemed good enough for play to continue, and, with no further breaks, England reached 49 without loss by the close, a lead of 30.

The third day witnessed one of those dramatic changes of fortune for which no easy explanation is forthcoming. One moment, it seemed,

---

*Both men bowled leg-breaks and 'googlies' at something near medium pace, but whereas Wright, more conventionally, kept the googly as a variant, O'Reilly at some stage of his career, had gone over to using the googly as his stock ball, with the occasional leg-break, which he tended to 'roll'.

England were moving steadily along at 60 for one, Edrich being the man out, and, with wickets in hand, were looking to set Australia the sort of target in tricky conditions, which, in difficult conditions, might prove beyond them. Then three things happened, each in themselves insignificant. First, Bradman switched O'Reilly to the pavilion end; second, Hardstaff hooked that most fiery of bowlers for four; third, Umpire Chester thought to no-ball that same fiery bowler. Whether O'Reilly approved of the first action, there is no telling, but it is safe to assume that the last two did nothing to foster Anglo-Australian relations. His blood was up, and, in consequence, he became twice the bowler. More to the point, 60 for one became 123 all out, as O'Reilly (five for 56) and Fleetwood-Smith (four for 34) unceremoniously swept aside the cream of English batting, leaving Australia with the nominal task of making 105 to win — and thereby retain the Ashes.

O'Reilly was known to have been furious at that hook and 'no-balling', and subsequently bowled like a man possessed. Such things you did to the Tiger at your peril, and it was England who lived to rue the day, though the excitement was not yet quite over. Australia lost both openers for nine apiece, and then the vital wickets of Bradman (16) and McCabe (15), and, at 50 for four, were in some trouble until Lindsay Hassett took command. Barnett, making his second important contribution of the match, gave staunch support, and, although Hassett went just before the end, Australia finally got home by the comfortable margin of five wickets. But they had lived dangerously, and had either Hassett or Barnett gone quickly, it might have been a very different story.

And who was it that brought panic to the Australian ranks? The long neglected Doug Wright, of course. The man thought to be too big a risk in the first innings dismissed Bradman, McCabe and Hasset in the second, at a cost to himself of 26 runs, which, of course, convinced his supporters all the more that Hammond had erred. In fairness, I do not think he was so much guilty of misjudgment, as of allowing his obsession with safety-first tactics to dictate his movements — or lack of them. In fact, few Test captains take chances, but, as we say, it was not what he did that brought criticism, but that he appeared to do little at all. Hammond the batsman and Hammond the captain, were two rather different beings. For all his glorious strokes, he had failed in his first quest for the Ashes; had Hammond known it, it would be eight years before he was granted a second chance.

So Leeds again proved a bogie ground for England (it was to know an even blacker day in 1948) and as is often the case, it was their strongest department, the much vaunted batting that had let them down. This was not their best side, of course, but the fact remained that four first choices, Barnett, Edrich, Compton and Paynter did almost nothing between them. Again, you could say that most of Australia's batsmen had fared little better, and that on a pitch where no innings reached 250, the bowlers had had conditions *too* much in their favour. Yet, two points can be set against this. First, we have Bill O'Reilly's testimony that the wicket was never unduly helpful to spin, and, to argue that this was possibly the jaundiced view of a bowler, is to have a poor conception of a man little given to embellishment. But perhaps the most convincing pointer was that the foremost batsman on either side, Hammond and Bradman, both showed that runs could be made if one possessed the necessary virtues, which, as we have stressed a hundred times, is surely the criterion of a fair balance between bat and ball. Every bowler had hope; the best on the day, took the wickets — yet the prize scalps still had to be earned, and Bradman, of course, was not renowned as a bad-wicket batsman. It can also be stressed that Ben Barnett, a world ranking wicket-keeper, yet hardly in that class with the bat, had twice demonstrated that with grit and application a batsman could survive. And why some of the more talented players did not make a better showing will ever remain a burning question.

There was no mystery, however, about the major reason why England, the 'stronger side', found themselves trailing at this stage — the presence of Don Bradman, as feared, had outweighed all the apparent strengths and advantages of the home team. It cannot be overstated just how much Australia owed their present position to Bradman, both as batsman and leader. Three times he had lost the toss, yet, at the first smell of victory, he had seized eagerly upon it. Here, whether relevant or not, his switching of O'Reilly to the other end, had spelled the beginning of disaster for England. Naturally though, it was Bradman's batting that Australia looked to most. A side in which only he and Brown showed any sort of consistency, obviously relied heavily upon them. Apart from that one magnificent innings of McCabe's, no one else made a century. Unlike previous tours, when Bradman had made capital from the solid starts of Woodful and Ponsford, he never once came in now with runs on the board, and while he did not run riot as of old, all three of his Test hundreds were made at crucial junctures, when every run counted. In the two matches where England had outscored Australia, Bradman twice played saving second-innings knocks; then, when England faltered in the Headingley mist, his 103 was the lynch-pin of a first-innings total that formed the platform for

Australia's victory. Once again the Bradman factor — for which no one could legislate — had outweighed the best that England could put into the field. Yet it was ironic that on the only occasion they shortened the batting, England met with the worst conditions of the series. A seventh batsman here might well have saved the match.

And so to the Oval — and a statistician's paradise. If runs and records were your delight, then Kennington, August 1938, was the place to be. The fate of the Ashes was no longer in question, but England could still square the rubber and at least preserve their pride. Accordingly, with the timeless element in mind, the selectors, learning from the lessons of Leeds, picked the strongest batting side yet. With Ames still unavailable, however, the extra batsman — Leyland at long last — could be brought in only at the expense of a bowler, and that bowler, need one say, was Doug Wright. It is strange how England have always tended to be suspicious of the leg-spinner, using them sparingly and as something of a luxury. Australia, for their part, have seen them as match-winners, and until recent years, seldom went into a Test match without one.

Fred Price, who had kept wicket at Headingley, was forced to drop out at the last moment, and a late summons went out to Yorkshire's Arthur Wood. Elated at this unexpected honour, Wood celebrated the award of his first cap at the age of forty by coming all the way by taxi, at a cost of a cool fiver. As a batsman, he was not quite in Ames's class, but he made his fifties, and his inclusion did not greatly lengthen the tail.

Less logical were the final batting deliberations. With Hutton now fit to resume and Leyland coming in at number three, someone would have to be left out. The obvious choice was Edrich who had yet to top thirty in five innings. An alternative was to drop him to a less onerous position in the order and omit Hardstaff, who had just the one game at Leeds. In fact, they retained Edrich in the opener's berth and left out Barnett, a decision which, in view of his rapid hundred on a similar wicket at Nottingham, seemed a strange one indeed, though, as time told, it could scarcely be considered costly.

In any event, it was certainly not nearly so unfortunate as that taken by Australia, though in fairness, their error was more in the nature of a calculated gamble that just didn't come off. No doubt feeling that Bradman was due to win the toss, they brought in the recovered Sid

Barnes for his first Test, and left out McCormick, effectively their only fast bowler. As we know, Bradman called wrongly yet again, which meant that a sadly depleted attack was faced with the unenviable task of bowling at a long, and strong batting side given first use of the wicket. And what a wicket! Like Trent Bridge, the Oval was a bowler's graveyard, and, in the 'thirties, perhaps even the more lifeless of the two. (Might not Jim Laker, had he played his cricket then, have been just another trundler?) O'Reilly said that he could smell the top-dressing* a mile away and he had good grounds to view his mission with foreboding. And McCormick was the unlucky one?

It is hard to imagine a more dispiriting experience than bowling on a hot day in these conditions to batsmen with all the time in the world at their disposal. Yet O'Reilly must have thought his luck had changed when he trapped Edrich leg before wicket for 12; this was his hundredth wicket against England, and now the fourth time he had claimed twenty in a series against them. Not that Edrich could have taken much pleasure from those statistics. How galling this latest failure must have seemed to him — a wicket full of runs, time of no consequence, and the chance — perhaps his last — gone begging. While it is easy to be wise after the event, of course, one must ask whether he was every really an opener.

There was no disputing Hutton's aptitude for the role, though; here was a young man with all the discipline, temperament and technique of a veteran. He was in no doubt as to what was expected of him† — to dig in, make a hundred, and dig in again. Hobbs and others often threw their wickets away on reaching three figures, their job done. Not Hutton. He had been brought up in the hard ways of Yorkshire cricket, and particularly by Sutcliffe, who was not impressed by that sort of thing. Once, when a young prodigy sought to indulge himself late in his innings, Sutcliffe walked down the pitch to him and said: "We don't play this game for fun, you know." Neither, in that sense, did Hutton play for fun, which does not mean he did not enjoy his cricket, simply that he took it seriously.

Now joined by fellow Yorkshireman Leyland, whom he knew so well and liked batting with, Hutton soon settled into a groove that promised little fun for the Australians either. Leyland, at 38, much the senior player, must have been a reassuring sight at the other end. Equally resolute and dedicated to the cause, he was also a fine judge of a run,

---

*Cow dung! Or in the more poetic terms of O'Reilly, 'Cowyard confetti'.
†Hammond, in fact, gave orders to his openers that he did not want to see them back before teatime; he felt he could not breathe easily until the score had passed six hundred.

and, slowly, the partnership thrived; at lunch England were 89 for one, and, shortly before tea, both men reached their centuries. It is interesting to note that, although this was a timeless match, where the general impression was of slow play, Hutton's century came up in three-and-a-half hours — not at all bad going by Test standards. Nor could 347 runs in a day be considered tardy progress, Hutton having made 160 and Leyland 156.

The day had not been without its qualms, however. Both batsmen might have been stumped during the afternoon session. Again, a thundery shower at the tea-interval delayed the restart for several minutes, and, though not sufficient to affect the wicket, the suspicion that it might have lingered for a while. And then, as the evening shadows lengthened, there was the fear that batsmen who had been in since early morning might lose concentration in the tricky light. Had a wicket fallen then, it could so easily have become two or three. Hammond was not the only one relieved that Hutton and Leyland saw out the day together.

The Saturday start meant a long wait until Monday, by which time the thundery heat of the first day had given way to much cooler, unsettled weather. Rain held up the start for thirty-five minutes, but, soon after, the mid-day sun broke through, and the long partnership was again under way. Already, they had broken all current records for the second wicket by Englishmen, and at the start had been only five runs short of the 323 of Hobbs and Rhodes — the highest for any wicket. This landmark was duly passed, and, as the morning wore on, with Hutton and Leyland in no kind of trouble, Bradman must have despaired as to where the next wicket was coming from. However, there is an old cricket maxim that when all else fails, bowl for run-outs. Whether this thought entered the great Australian's mind is rather doubtful, but, nevertheless, at ten minutes to one, Leyland forgot another old maxim, 'Never run for a mis-field' and, attempting a second from Hasset's fumble, was run out by a combination of that fielder's swift return and smart backing up by the captain himself. The score was now 411 for two; Leyland had made 187; the second wicket had put on 382.

Having taken nearly seven hours to achieve that breakthrough, the sight of Hammond coming through the gate was enough to discourage the most doughty of spirits. Nor could Australia have taken much heart from the knowledge that when Hammond had had his fill, Paynter, Compton and Hardstaff were all waiting to feast off the carcass. Meanwhile, of course, they had still to dispose of Hutton, who, in this form, looked good for a week. As McCabe, preparing to bowl, remarked to the umpire: "Geez! They'll get a thousand."

That prognostication did not look to be far off the mark, as Hammond, remarkably at ease for a man who had spent two days with his pads on, took 12 off the first over, and at lunch, England were strongly placed at 434 for two, Hutton 191, Hammond 20. Many here, though, remembered that on this ground four years earlier, just two Australians had made more than that between them. There was still a long way to go before English hearts could rest easy.

Bradman had held back the new ball until after the interval, and, in the first hour of the afternoon, in which the Australians stuck well to their task, scoring was restricted to 43 runs. However, slowing things down in a timeless match is ultimately to no advantage, and before long, Bradman was again seeking desperately for a wicket. Hutton was now well past 200 after eight-and-a-half hours at the crease, and not since Saturday afternoon could one recall him giving a semblance of a chance. Soon Hammond too, was timing his strokes sweetly, reaching 50 with a glorious cover-drive that boded ill for the fielding side. The 500 came and went. Hutton reached 250, passing Hammond's record 240, set two months earlier, of the highest individual score against Australia in England. Bradman was now completely on the defensive, even Fleetwood-Smith and O'Reilly bowling without a slip. The sight of the ever-hostile Irishman reduced to a toothless Tiger, said something for Australia's plight.

Yet, with England 546 for two, a stand of 135 in progress and a wealth of batting to come, Bradman's generalship in the field, and his unflagging efforts to keep his team on their toes, was no less evident than it had been on Saturday morning. This perseverence was to be rewarded; the break Australia so badly wanted was now forthcoming.

Shortly before tea, with the sun shining brightly, Hammond, on 59, looked to be well in command when, uncharacteristically, he played across the line to Fleetwood-Smith, missed, and was adjudged leg before wicket. This was disappointing for the crowd, of course, but hardly a disaster otherwise — yet. He had barely left the crease, however, when rumblings were heard overhead, and the sky, clear a moment before, suddenly darkened as ominous thunder clouds gathered over the ground. This was not the best time for a new batsman to come in, especially on a ground where batsmen find difficulty picking up the ball's flight against the grey background. Paynter, given no chance to accustom his eyes to the light, probably did not see the leg-break from O'Reilly which, a few balls later, had him leg-before. 546 for four; last man 0, and still a few overs to go to tea.

Compton came in with strict orders to stay until the interval, which he managed to do — just. During tea, the threatened storm that would have saved Paynter, erupted. Though it was soon over, the light was still far from good when play resumed at five o'clock. Bradman, alert as ever to the problems confronting the batsmen, and sensing that here was his chance to keep England's score within reasonable bounds, brought on his quickest bowler, Waite, at the pavilion end. Compton had probably the best eye among English cricketers; but he too was deceived by the wide-armed delivery coming from out of the shadows, and played over the top to be clean bowled for one. 546 for two had become 555 for five; England were down to their last accredited batsman, Hardstaff, and, in this light, who knew how long he might hold out. Hutton was still there, of course, his eyes adjusted to the gloom, but, after ten hours batting, his frail form was almost spent. Never of strong constitution, he had stood through every ball since the start, and was now playing as if from memory, wearily going through the motions. If he got out, England might be lucky to reach 600. Australia's tenacity had put them back in the game. Much depended on the next hour's play.

If Paynter and Compton could be counted unlucky, then, in marked contrast, fortune smiled on Hardstaff. No sooner had his god-like figure reached the crease, than the clouds gave way to blue skies and sunshine, as if in celebration of the radiant nature of his cricket. Almost at once he was playing his shots, stroking the ball around the field with a flashing blade. You would not have guessed that Hardstaff was batting in a timeless Test where only he stood between the Australian bowlers and the tail, or that he had come in after the fall of three quick wickets. If he had received any special briefing, it was not patently obvious.

Hutton meanwhile simply went on and on, his concentration seemingly endless. Though weary almost to the point of collapse, he scarcely played a false stroke, and certainly gave no palpable chance. The crowd fell silent as he approached R. E. Foster's historic 287, a milestone that marked the highest score by an Englishman in Anglo-Australian Tests. A moment later the Oval rang to the echo, as the cheers announced to all of South London that 'Hutton had done it'. Hardly less deafening was the applause that greeted his 300 just before the close. Could he now go on to beat Bradman's all-comer's record of 334? That was the big talking point when Hutton and Hardstaff came in undefeated at the end of an enthralling day's play.

England were 634 for five, Hardstaff 40, with the feared collapse averted, and, despite stoppages, a period of poor light and a mini-crisis, 287 runs had come in roughly even time. The magic total of 1,000 was again a possibility. Hutton would start fresh next morning, while Hardstaff had batted in a manner that gave promise of much more to come. If, inevitably, the prospect of a new world record claimed most of our attention, the morrow gave much else to contemplate — not least, that the longest innings in first-class cricket was about to enter its third day.

A crowd of some 30,000 turned up at the Oval on the Tuesday morning, and it is a safe bet that 29,500 of them came to see Hutton break Bradman's record. Could he do it? He was tantalisingly close, but a good few fingernails would part company with their owners before — and if — that time arrived. The certainty was that Bradman would do Hutton no favours, would try by every fair means — physical and psychological — to prise him out. Indeed, it was surely both poignant and rare for the holder and challenger of such a record to be in direct conflict. Thirty-five more runs when one already has 300 may seem trifling, but, as Hutton himself well knew, every one of those runs would cost dear in physical and nervous strain. Already he had paid a price for his long vigil. Hutton always lost weight during a cricket season; in the course of this innings he shed half a stone. Even a night's rest had left him jaded and aching in every muscle, the stiffness still with him when he came to the ground. To add to his troubles, the broken finger which had kept him out of Leeds was visibly swollen and giving some discomfort. But aches and pains or no, Hutton's moment had arrived.

His appearance that morning was no occasion for the polite ripple of applause that is normally accorded incoming batsmen. As he and Hardstaff walked out, the huge, partisan crowd clapped the Yorkshireman all the way to the wicket — a nation and their hero, willing him to that record. For the moment, the state of the match was forgotten, that contest now secondary. But what if our champion should go in the first over, or, even worse perhaps, fail by just a run or two? It did not bear thinking about. Hutton, one suspects, was under less strain that the spectators; he had more to occupy his mind.

Bradman was not going to risk playing him in with medium-paced seam, and began straightway with the spin of O'Reilly and Fleetwood-Smith, in any case his front-line bowlers. Thus, inevitably, pressure was put upon Hutton from the start. Yet it was strange that although Fleetwood-Smith spun from leg, as too occasionally did O'Reilly, no slip was posted for either, the attack being directed at leg-stump with three men in close-catching positions on the leg-side. Clearly, Bradman hoped that by restricting Hutton's productive off-side strokes, he would oblige him either to look for runs through the leg-side cordon, or wait for the loose delivery. Only by taking risks could he force on the off-side, which, of course, was exactly what Bradman intended.

Hutton, however, was in no hurry. He had all day if necessary in which to make the runs, and eleven hours patient grafting was not going to be tossed away through a sudden rush of blood to the head. His first run, a single on the on-side, was greeted with a long burst of applause, which did something to relieve the tension. Hardstaff, too, got his score moving again with a two and a single in the second over, and soon went on to his fifty, made in one hundred minutes. He proved a good foil for Hutton at this time, keeping the score ticking over while his partner concentrated mainly on defence. Hutton's first five scoring-strokes were all singles from leg-side pushes and deflections, yet the crowd cheered his every run, as, indeed, they had come to do. He did not always look certain during this opening spell — was twice rapped on the plad by Fleetwood-Smith, and once popped one up perilously close to the lurking short-legs. Bradman, sensing a possible weakness, crossed over to bolster the leg-trap. Thus warned, Hutton now played well forward, bat angled to smother the spin, waiting for the one that strayed off line. Soon Fleetwood-Smith overpitched, and Hutton drove him through the off-side field for his first four of the day, all the Oval urging it over the boundary.

That stroke brought up the hundred partnership, the third of the innings, with Hutton, needless to say, having figured in all three. But every long innings needs its luck. Shortly after twelve o'clock, Hutton had made 315 when O'Reilly got one to turn sufficiently to find the edge of the bat. It would have been a straightforward catch to slip, but there was no slip. O'Reilly tore at his balding scalp in despair as the ball trickled harmlessly down to third man — but should he, in any case, have been bowling without one? Fortunate there, Hutton was then beaten by one from Fleetwood-Smith that only narrowly missed the off stump. Another nasty moment. Bradman, getting no joy from his spinners, called for the fourth new ball.

The decision was really forced upon him. With his spinners already doing double-duty, and with few other options, Bradman had delayed taking the new ball simply because he had no one of penetration to use it. Yet, tense as was the morning struggle, 40 runs had come in the first forty-five minutes and England were 674 for five. The game had steadily swung back England's way, giving Bradman a two-fold problem. Not only was his record in jeopardy, but, more important Australia could soon be facing a total that was beyond reach. With Hardstaff playing the spinners easily, and Hutton for the most part content to push forward, he had to try some way of unsettling them. He may also have been influenced by the heavy cloud which had been building up since the start. This might enable Waite and McCabe, to whom he now turned, to move the ball in the air.

In fact, the scoring rate increased and, after only three overs, Bradman brought back O'Reilly, now bowling though, to a purely defensive field. Hutton could take the odd single, but boundaries were effectively denied him. Inspired by the captain, the fielding, it should be said, was first-class throughout. Bradman, we know, was naturally keen to preserve his record, but, above all, he was leading his country against England. In this cause, his active example in the field, his constant striving to outwit batsman, his attention to field placings and detail generally, never wavered. At no time during this long innings — not even when England were 400 for one with Hutton and Leyland apparently set for eternity — did he give less than one hundred per cent, something which applied to the whole team. Effort that had not flagged under dire pressure was now redoubled in defence of his record.

Nevertheless, by degrees, Hutton drew nearer the target, at length beating the field with a delicate late cut for four to take his score to 321. Hardstaff meanwhile, continued to give vigorous support and after an hour's play which produced sixty runs, England were 694 for five, Hardstaff 77. Another single to Hutton, and then with the best stroke of the day, he seized on a shortish ball from Waite and cut it hard off the back foot to the third man boundary. Three hundred and twenty-six. Nine more runs would do it. The crowd prepared itself mentally. Most needed reminding that the stroke had brought up the 700.

A single towards the end of the over, and another off the next from O'Reilly took Hutton to 328. The time had come for Bradman's last throw. Of all his bowlers, Fleetwood-Smith was the one most likely to produce the unplayable ball, the one capable of beating the defensive stroke of a batsman thoroughly set. Bradman, arch-strategist that he was, had kept him back for the psychological moment. With only seven runs wanted, and tension at boiling point, that moment had surely arrived.

With Hutton so close to the record, Bradman rightly reasoned that with the field spread wide, he was almost certain to get there eventually. His best hope lay in crowding the bat, forcing Hutton to fetch his runs, with any false stroke likely to go to hand. Under such pressure, and in an atmosphere that stretched nerves to the limit, even one of Hutton's cool temperament might be forced into error.

In the circumstances — Hutton's tender years, twenty-two be it remembered, the occasion, the duration of his innings — it is doubtful if any batsman has ever been subjected to a more testing ordeal. Eight men clustered round the bat as Fleetwood-Smith came in from the pavilion end, just the one fielder at cover not in a close-catching position. Spare a thought, too, for the bowler whose lot it was either to dismiss the batsman at the eleventh hour, or concede him the necessary runs. This was no time for the loose delivery; no less than Hutton, Fleetwood-Smith needed all his concentration, as well as cool nerve, in order to drop the ball on the spot. Yet few consider the bowler's feelings at such times.

Bradman, alert to every ploy, had switched his spinners over so that Fleetwood-Smith might have the benefit of bowling from out of the darker background. The gambit almost paid off. Hutton was late picking up his first delivery and, in playing back, was rapped on the pads. Our hearts went into our mouths. "Howzat!" yelled ten frenzied fieldsmen, arms upstretched.

"Not out," answered Umpire Chester, unmoved. A shade too high.

If Fleetwood-Smith was affected by the heavy onus upon him, he did not show it. Right on a length, extracting both spin and bounce from a lifeless pitch, it was all Hutton could do to smother his next two deliveries. Now, the fourth ball beat him all ends up, again rapping him on the pads, and again he was bang in front. Thirty thousand hearts stopped as one. He had to be out this time surely. The men in green caps were in no doubt as they turned triumphantly to Frank Chester. "Howzat!" they chorused.

It is almost certain, with no disrespect to an honest and conscientious body of men, that any other umpire would have upheld the appeal. Chester, however, was Chester. He was, without argument, the doyen of umpires, and probably the most respected of those who ever stood in a Test match. A keen eye is, of course, a prerequisite for the job, but he was also possessed of phenomenal hearing. Here, those wonderful ears had detected the faintest of tickles as the ball brushed Hutton's bat en route to the pad. "Not out," he adjudged, a verdict that, if disappointing to the Australians, assured him of the undying gratitude of a relieved crowd — and Hutton too, we think. Two hair's breadth decisions in four balls was more than flesh and blood could stand.

Never has a crowd been so pleased to see the end of an over as it was when Fleetwood-Smith took his cap. One could almost feel the release of breath in the concerted sigh that went up around the Oval. Hutton managed a single from each of the next three overs, to take his score to 331. One good hit would do it.

O'Reilly had two more balls of his over left before Hutton would again face Fleetwood-Smith, and to the first of these he put all his weight into what looked to be a reckless swing to leg. He missed completely, but, as we might have guessed, a no-ball had been called. Yet O'Reilly was so accurate, that Hutton was unable to take advantage.

Hardstaff took a single off Fleetwood-Smith's next over, to bring Hutton down to the striker's end. It is no mere figure of speech to say that everyone was on the edge of their seat, as, in an atmosphere charged with emotion, Fleetwood-Smith came in for what one sensed was his final fling, one way or the other. We could not have stood it much longer. Nor, it seemed, could Hutton. The ball, straight, but a trifle short, was the one he had been waiting for. It was perhaps now or never. Stepping outside leg-stump to give himself room for the cut, Hutton met the ball with the full force of a down-swept bat, wrists turning on impact to send it racing past point to the boundary. No one moved, and it would not have mattered if they had. It was four from the moment it left the bat. Hutton had broken the record, and had done it in style.

I was not present at the Oval in 1882 when a spectator died of excitement and another gnawed clean through his umbrella; but I'll wager that seldom can there have been scenes such as we saw here, as hats, cushions, and anything else that came to hand, were thrown high in the air amid cheering reminiscent of Mafeking night. And who was the first to congratulate Hutton on his wonderful achievement? No less than the man who had worked hardest to deny him — Don Bradman, an unyielding and often ruthless opponent, but one always generous in praise of other's merit. He recognised greatness when he saw it, and could take some consolation that his record had gone to a worthy successor. Nor would Hutton now relax his vigilance — another characteristic he shared with the prolific Australian.

Had this been Denis Compton, say, little can be more certain that that, to the next ball, he would have gone down the wicket either to hit a boundary or to be stumped, and not much caring which. Or he may just possibly have lingered to take the two runs required to pass Hammond's all-Test record of 336 before giving it a thrash. But that was Compton. Never for a moment, even at this stage when he was both physically and mentally drained, could one imagine Hutton accelerating his own downfall. Like Bradman, he would go on batting all the time there was breath in his body. Certainly, no bowler would be made a present of his wicket. As both men might have said: "We do not play this game for fun."

Inevitably, there was a sense of anticlimax once Hutton had overtaken Hammond's record, and it was some while before new landmarks again gave the game meaning. We were thankful for Hardstaff's presence at this time; with anyone less attractive to watch, or less willing to go for their shots, interest would certainly have waned. From the time he came in, Hardstaff was, at best, destined to play a supporting role, yet had he failed, the scenes we had just witnessed might never have happened at all. But how well he had figured in this long and productive partnership — first to help England through a crisis, then to take the pressure off Hutton, and later as his partner neared the record, to give him as much of the strike as possible.

Now, Hardstaff was rewarded with his own hundred, and, shortly afterwards, his stand with Hutton reached 200, easily an English record for the sixth wicket in Tests. With Hutton so firmly entrenched at the other end, there seemed no reason why they should ever be parted, but, with his score 364, sheer fatigue caused Hutton to loft a drive to cover, giving O'Reilly his third wicket of the innings. Hutton had batted for thirteen hours and twenty minutes, hit 35 fours, figured in two record breaking partnerships, and seen England from nil to 770 for six.

Any faint hopes Australia might have entertained that Hutton's dismissal would bring an end to the slaughter were sadly misplaced. Hammond had no intention of giving them so much as a hint of a procurable total, and Wood came in with orders simply to carry on the good work. But then came one of the unforeseeable calamities that render all calculations void. With the score nearing 800, the bowling had virtually melted away, and soon everyone who could do so was turning an arm. Now, Bradman took the ball himself, but in the run up, turned his foot in a rut worn deep by the bowler's poundings, breaking a small bone in the ankle. He slumped to the ground, his players clustering round him, and then, after some delay, was carried from the field amid a hubbub of consternation. A sad sight, that summed up Australia's current fortunes all too well. Patriot or not, it would have been a hard man indeed who felt no sympathy for the departing skipper — and his team. In a match where almost nothing had gone right for them, Bradman had for two-and-a-half days given himself wholly to the task entrusted to him. Now, when more than ever, Australia were in need of his batting, a cruel twist of fate had robbed them of his services. With him, they would have been hard enough pressed to come within reach of England's mammoth total; without him, and another late casualty, Fingleton, the substance had gone from their possible counter. Which for English folk, too, was far from satisfactory.

Suddenly, it was not fun any more. Any elation one might have felt at the prospect of our Headingley conquerors being soundly whipped was now clouded by possible suggestion of a hollow victory. This would not, of course, have been quite fair since England had already played themselves into a vastly strong position before Bradman's departure. Yet most people prefer to win fairly and squarely against full-strength opponents, and that was now no longer possible. In fact, to a sporting public not known for its ruthless instincts, to hammer a side shorn of their champion almost smacked of kicking a man when he's down. In some quarters it was felt that Hammond's relentless pursuit of runs was carried too far. Which makes one think that, at times, a captain's lot is indeed a thankless one.

So the massacre went on. Hardstaff reached 150, and Wood further celebrated his selection by making 50 at the first time of asking. His dismissal at 857 for seven gave rise to one of cricket's favourite quips. On entering the pavilion, Wood shook his head and sighed: "Trust me to get out in a crisis."

And still no declaration, which at this stage of proceedings, *was* perhaps carrying caution to extremes. Hardstaff was nowhere near 200, and Verity was apparently sent in only to pile on the agony. More likely, though, this was just another example of Hammond 'letting the game go on'. However, he did not allow it to drift for much longer. When, with the 900 up, it looked as though England would bat on to the bitter end, Hammond called a halt to Australia's suffering by declaring at 903 for seven, Hardstaff 169 not out. At last, it was over — easily the highest score in Test cricket, and likely to remain so. We had, for sure, witnessed history in the making.

That, from the outset, conditions heavily favoured the bat was borne out by the bowling figures of O'Reilly and Fleetwood-Smith. In all-round terms, O'Reilly was probably the best bowler in the world, and certainly the most aggressive, yet, without ever being taken apart, finished with a return of three for 178. Fleetwood-Smith, though less consistent, was nevertheless good enough to twice come near to dismissing Hutton when his score had exceeded 300. His reward? One for 298! These figures hardly did justice to either. Between them they got through 172 overs, and O'Reilly whose overs cost roughly two apiece, succeeded in sending down 26 maidens. But, in the end, the wicket ground them into the dust.

Yet, only three batsmen made the most of their opportunity, and the score-card makes remarkably uneven reading. It might almost provide a cryptic quiz teaser. 'If Edrich made 12, Compton 1, and Paynter not quite so many, what was England's score?' Such clues do not readily suggest 903 for seven. But, if several missed the boat here, what can one make of Australia's utter failure to offer more than token resistance when their turn came to bat?

No wholly satisfactory explanation can be found. Granted that they were without their chief run-getter, plus another front-line batsman; granted too, that after the best part of three days in the field they faced a most dispiriting task that was always beyond them; and, granted again, that Farnes and Bowes got far more out of the wicket than Australia's pace bowlers had done — still none of these things quite explains why, on a wicket which had seen record after record broken, a side still well-stocked with batting, could scrape together totals no larger than 201 and 123, thus meeting defeat by the record margin of an innings and 579 runs. My belief, for what it's worth, is that the timeless element killed all incentive. Short of batting through until September, Australia had nothing whatsoever to play for, not even a grim, backs-to-the-wall draw — which would have been a worthy aim in their position. Only a monsoon could save them, and, for all, the quirks of our weather, we don't get too many of those. The idea of ensuring a finish seemed at first glance a good one, but, as became clear, timeless Tests made for cricket without drama — which is rather like Hamlet without a Ghost.

Not too much can be said of the Australian batting, but Farnes and Bowes bowled well on a still plumb wicket, their extra pace extracting a lift not evident while Waite and McCabe were operating. Of course, it is a great psychological boost bowling with a big total behind you — and they certainly had that — yet, even so, this was an abrupt and disappointing ending to a match that at one stage had promised to roll on until Christmas. As ever, conjecture was endless. How many might Bradman have made on a ground where his previous two visits had brought him double-centuries? Where would England have been without Hutton's marathon innings? And so on. Of course, no one knows how many Bradman would have made, though one could guess, but one has a feeling that had Hutton scored rather less runs that he did, someone else — Hammond, Paynter, Compton — would have played a big innings. A long stand is always difficult to follow, and batsmen who have waited long for their turn, are often prey to this situation. Compton, in particular, was a retriever of causes rather than one who cashed in on flying starts, and, in general, was not seen at his best when there were already runs on the board. But that is pure hypothesis. What one can say, with a fair amount of conviction, as already intimated, is that the concept of timeless Tests was not a success. One detraction we have just mentioned, but another is that the luck of the toss is too likely to dictate the outcome. On good wickets, batting first is an advantage in any circumstances. In timeless matches, where scores tend to be larger and teams are kept longer in the field, the penalty of losing the toss is that much greater, and often decisive — as Bradman, O'Reilly and the rest would no doubt heartily agree.

Nevertheless. an anticlimax or not, the Oval match was not likely to be forgotten in a hurry and, of course, it never has been. The fact that it was the last timeless Test to be played in this country alone marks it historically, while many of the records set up hold good to this day. True, Hutton's innings was eventually eclipsed both numerically and in terms of duration by Sobers and Hanif respectively, but it is still unsurpassed in matches against Australia. Records are made to be broken, but the fact that they sometimes are in no way diminishes the occasion of their first making. Should Hutton's score be exceeded a dozen times, it was still the highest then, and that is the best that can be achieved. Those present witnessed a unique event; that impression can never be taken from them, and is surely the stuff from which memories are made. Moreover, they can still relate that they saw the highest innings total in Test match history, and, unless playing conditions drastically change, are in little danger of having that boast denied them.

No one would pretend, overall, that this was a tensely exciting series. There were none of the cliff-hanging finishes of, say, 1902; nor was it the close-fought oscillatory contest of 1955. What we saw here, though, was a feast of individual display; high moments of either exceptional brilliance or singular achievement — beginning with Barnett's 99 before lunch on the very first morning, and ending with the historic events of the Oval. Between times there was McCabe's inspired onslaught at Trent Bridge, a composition of pure Hammond at Lords, while, predictably, Bradman three times rose to the occasion with masterfully engineered centuries. If you added the not inconsiderable contributions of Brown, O'Reilly, Paynter, Compton and Hardstaff, it is quite plain that, whatever the shortcomings of the rubber as a thrilling contest, it did not want for memorable incident or cricketing excellence.

Not least, of course, this series is remembered for the Wagnerian scale of its run-scoring. Everything was bigger and better than before. In fact, had one known it, the run feast had all but reached saturation point. Six months later, the infamous Durban Test, that dragged on for ten days and still remained unfinished, spelt the end of timeless Tests and their concomitant scores. Huge totals and records hold a certain novelty interest, but, when they follow as a matter of course, with the bowler made incidental to the game, their making is inevitably devalued.

Not that Hutton's epic was anything but a monumental effort of concentration, technical accomplishment and physical endurance. To bat through two days and more, with interruptions, against bowlers of the quality of O'Reilly and Fleetwood-Smith, even on that most placid of wickets, called for application far beyond the norm. Yet, Hutton himself does not rate it his best innings, and, in truth, it was not one that many would choose as one of their eight Desert Island videos. It was something one saw once, savoured at the time, but would not relish having every day. Not that we are now likely to have the chance.

With or without a war, those days — brought on largely by the influence of Bradman — were numbered. Timeless tests became pointless exercises where runs chased yet more runs as captains sought to ensure against defeat. Only when the drawn game at Durban reached unbelievably tedious proportions — Van der Byl and Gibb each taking seven hours over their hundreds — was it thought time to call a halt. There would still be slow play when the need arose, of course, but not purely for the sake of it. The monster had finally devoured itself.

As one might expect, the Australian visit tended to overshadow all else that summer, though, in any case, the Test matches apart, a season that began with both Edrich and Bradman making 1,000 runs before the end of May never quite lived up to that early promise. Nevertheless, as with most years, 1938 had its high moments. In fact, the county championship, as in the fifties, was not so much lack-lustre as all-too predictable — Yorkshire, almost as of right, taking the title for the sixth time in eight years. They lost only two matches, which, in view of Test calls — there were five White Rose men on duty at the Oval — plus injuries to Hutton and Leyland, was a fine achievement and said much for their reserve strength.

They were ably led by the amateur Brian Sellers, a man wholly devoted to Yorkshire's cause, who, in nine playing seasons spanning the war years, took them to six championships. Like many an amateur skipper of those days, Sellers would not perhaps have made the side strictly on merit, yet he was no mean batsman, fielded superbly, possessed a shrewd tactical brain, and, above all, won his team's loyalty because he showed so much of that quality himself. Anyway, in that side, it was not necessary for Sellars to make more than useful contributions with the bat. Apart from their current England men, the veteran Sutcliffe was still going strong, a model of consistency who rarely knew a poor season. His critics claimed that he was a batsman of limited strokes, which may have been true, but there was nothing limited about Sutcliffe's ability. Anyone who makes over 50,000 runs in twenty years must be equipped with a boundary shot or two, and neither Yorkshire nor England saw fit to complain that such strokes were overworked.

But if Sutcliffe, Hutton and Leyland were the big names in the batting, Wilf Barber and Arthur Mitchell might well have had more than eight caps between them in a less prosperous era. Yardley too, the Cambridge Blue* of a year or two back, and a future England captain, was now in his second full season with the county, and so, with Sellars to follow, plus handy runs from Wood and Verity, the batting was well taken care of.

By Yorkshire standards, but only by Yorkshire standards, the bowling was slightly less strong than in days gone by. Bowes and Verity were England cricketers who need no further commendation, but, apart from off-spinner Ellis Robinson, the attack was largely shared by their several all rounders. Frank Smailes, who a year later was to take ten wickets in an innings against Derbyshire, Leyland with his 'chinamen', Mitchell off-breaks, and Yardley, medium cutters, all played their part in a versatile bowling attack. It is not for me, a mere outsider, to say whether this side compared favourably with its predecessors of the twenties or early nineteen-hundreds. All one knows is that it was the envy of every other county, and looked certain to dominate the championship for years to come. It took a world holocaust to bring a temporary end to Yorkshire supremacy.

Middlesex, fast developing into a side to challenge the best, finished runners-up, albeit by a distance. With the young hopes Edrich and Compton now launched upon international careers, the batting

---

*Yardley, resplendent in Cambridge trappings, appears at number 34 among those evergreen cigarette cards — still smiling with resigned good humour.

weakness created by Hendren's departure no longer existed. Compton's natural genius had in two years allowed him to make the transition from number eleven to Test cricketer, with scarcely a hiccup; while Edrich, for all his failures for England this summer, showed no such inhibitions at county level. His was purely a problem of temperament; his ability was never in question. These two, along with the highly promising Jack Robertson, were the oncoming youth expected to provide the main scoring power over the next decade or two. Walter Robins and Gubby Allen were Test all-rounders of long standing, men of great experience who had captained England. Sims also, at this stage of his career, was adept enough with both bat and ball to be picked for his country as an all-rounder.

Traditionally, Middlesex, from Bosenquet to Bedford have seldom wanted for top-class leg-spinners. Now, in Robins, Sims and another ex-England cap, Ian Peebles, they possessed three leg-break and googly merchants, who, together with Compton, originally played as a slow left-arm bowler, formed a most interesting, if slightly unconventional spin quartet. The only bowler of real pace was 'Big Jim' Smith, who incidentally made the record books this year, though not, as it happens, in a bowling capacity. Tall and strongly built, with a good eye, C. I. J. Smith, like other fast bowlers before him, was famed as a big-hitter. In 1938 he played two short, but sweet, whirlwind innings in fairly quick succession. Against Sussex at Lords, Smith hit 69 in twenty minutes and, ten days later, made 66 in eighteen minutes against Gloucestershire at Bristol, the first fifty coming in the record time of eleven minutes. It remains the fastest authentic fifty ever. Middlesex, as perhaps this indicates, were not just a good side, but thoroughly entertaining too.

Another fast bowler to make news for activities outside his chosen trade was Wellard. In 1936, this renowned big-hitter had taken 30 from an over of Derbyshire's T. Armstrong. He now went one better, hitting 31 (five 6s) off the great Frank Woolley in Somerset's match against Kent at Wells. Until Sobers managed a full 36 against Glamorgan in 1968, this was the most runs scored off a six-ball over.

One feat that can hardly be bettered, and is not even likely to be equalled, was that of Arthur Fagg in making two double-centuries in a match. Going in first for Kent against Essex at Brentwood, Fagg scored 244 in the first innings, and was still there with 202 not out at the end of the second. It was an incredible performance in which he scarcely left the field of play.

To say that this was a batsman's year is the master of

understatements. There have been other seasons — 1928 for instance — where the bat was seen to dominate, yet which nevertheless produced an outstanding bowling performance somewhere along the line. But well though some bowled this summer, one cannot recall a single exceptional bowling feat* — certainly nothing that found its way into the record books. No, the batsman had things almost all their own way, and, fittingly perhaps, none more so than the respective champions of their countries, Hammond and Bradman. Hammond topped the batting averages (for home players), scoring 3,011 runs (average 75.27) including 15 centuries. Bradman, in rather fewer innings, averaged 115.66, the highest three-figure average recorded at that time, and made 13 centuries. Runs, runs, runs — there seemed no end to it.

However, one should perhaps say that to view this season in isolation, from a perspective of nearly fifty years, is to see it out of context. This was merely the climax of an ever-increasing trend since the twenties, and thus at the time came as nothing too unusual. As we said at the beginning, people usually become inured to the cricket of their day, so that, apart from a few purists, and one suspects, rather more bowlers, the endless run orgy was a fairly acceptable diet. In the end, it comes down to personal choice. If, as it was to most, big was beautiful, then one had a field-day; if though, one felt for the bowlers, who at times seemed no more than lackeys, one might well have thought that matters had gone too far. In my view, it was fine while it lasted; a page of history; an experience one was glad to have known and shared, but not, one feels, the type of cricket that would keep one interested indefinitely. As an exhibition of batsmanship in all its moods and styles, it was all one could ask for; as a red-blooded, cut-and-thrust confrontation between batsman and bowler, it left something, if not everything, to be desired.

Whatever one says, however, 1938 saw a unique tide of events, which plainly offers one good reason why time has not dimmed its memory; yet this does not, we think, constitute the main reason for its nostalgic appeal. That, I rather fancy, has more to do with the year itself, and why, as we said, I am inclined to believe that distance has lent enchantment. There were so many things we could not know — for example, that this was to be the last normal, carefree summer in a long while. Cricket in 1939 was played under the threat of war, a war that in fact materialised before the season's end, and therein, for the latter

---

*Australia's McCormick did make news, of a kind, by bowling 19 no-balls in his first three overs of the tour!

part, the visiting West Indians had one eye on the boat that was to take them home.

All of which gave this last season an air of unreality; something that took place yet which seemed of little account. Thus, in restrospect, one tends to think of 1938 as the true end of the pre-war cricket era — the last time for ten years that we were to see an Australian side here. The last time altogether, that many an old favourite took part against them. Men like Sutcliffe, Leyland, Paynter, to mention but a few, would know premature retirement, too old at the war's end to make a come-back. Others, robbed of six good years, would be past their best, or, like Bowes, have had their health impaired through active service. More poignant yet, there were those who would not return — Verity, Farnes, that bastion of Glamorgan cricket, Major Turnbull, G. H. Chalk of Kent — these numbered among the thousands who gave their lives that we might again know a fair English cricket season, unclouded by tyranny; heroes gone beyond recall, their innings nobly played. On that count alone, is not 1938 deserving of a very special place in our affections? We surely think it is.

Epilogue

Our choice of five favourite summers is complete. Your choice may have differed from mine. Nevertheless, it would be surprising if our wavelengths have not crossed somewhere along the way. Whether among them, we have described 'A season for all men', if indeed there is such a thing, is another matter; the chances are that you will never please everybody. But let us not be too analytical; if you have got this far, then we must have much in common, for the very good reason that cricket is more than a game, more a way of life. As such, every season must bring its share of treats and pleasures. Indeed, at times, if all one could remember was the sun climbing over the stand to wend an unbroken arc across the ground, memories would be piquant enough.

To bask on such a day, lunchbox at your feet, fills one with a sense of well-being rarely encountered. The stands suggest a gay tapestry as summer frocks blend with shirt-sleeve order. Bathed in a golden radiance, a holiday crowd buzzes in expectation — good-humoured, solely on pleasure bent. The grass, dew-pearled, glistens in the morning sunlight, foretelling a day humming with heat. Score-cards for sale; cushions for hire — the vendors give forth a well-versed patter. Then sounds the bell — the hubbub subsides to a low murmur, signalling the umpires are on their way . . .

A portrait gallery of
British and
Australian Test Cricketers

M. LEYLAND
Yorkshire & England
B. 20/7/1900

E. PAYNTER
Lancashire & England
B. 5/11/1901

A. W. WELLARD
Somerset & England
B. 8/4/1903

W. R. HAMMOND
Glos & England
B. 19/6/1903

L. E. G. AMES
Kent & England
B. 3/12/1905

H. VERITY
Yorkshire & England
B. 18/5/1905

W. J. O'REILLY
NSW & Australia
B. 20/12/1905

E. L. McCORMICK
Victoria & Australia
B. 16/5/1906

B. A. BARNETT
Victoria
B. 23/3/1908

D. G. BRADMAN
NSW, South Australia
& Australia
B. 27/4/1908

L. O'B. FLEETWOOD-SMITH
Victoria & Australia
B. 30/3/1910

J. H. W. FINGLETON
NSW & Australia
B. 28/4/1908

C. J. BARNETT
Glos & England
B. 3/7/1910

S. J. McCABE
NSW & Australia
B. 16/7/1910

J. HARDSTAFF, Jnr.
Notts & England
B. 3/7/1911

K. BARNES
Cambs, Essex & England
B. 8/7/1911

H. G. WAITE
South Australia
B. 17/1/1911

A. L. HASSETT
Victoria
B. 28/8/1913

W. A. BROWN
NSW, Queensland
& Australia
B. 31/7/1912

W. J. EDRICH
Middlesex
B. 26/3/1916

L. HUTTON
Yorkshire & England
B. 23/6/1916

C. L. BADCOCK
S. Australia & Australia
B. 24/10/1914

S. BARNES
New South Wales
B. 5/6/1917

D. S. C. COMPTON
Middlesex & England
B. 23/5/1918

C. P. MEAD
Hampshire
B. 9/3/1887

H. SUTCLIFFE
Yorkshire
B. 25/11/1894

F. E. WOOLLEY
Kent
B. 27/5/1887

J. R. HOBBS
Surrey
B. 16/12/1882

C. HALLOWS
Lancashire
B. 4/4/1895

E. HENDREN
Middlesex
B. 5/2/1889

E. TYLDESLEY
Lancashire
B. Feb. 1889

A. P. FREEMAN
Kent
B. 17/5/1889

H. LARWOOD
Notts
B. 14/11/1904

W. R. HAMMOND
Glos
B. 19/6/1903

D. R. JARDINE
Surrey
B. 23/10/1900

L. AMES
Kent
B. 3/12/1905

C. DUCKWORTH
Lancashire
B. 9/5/1901